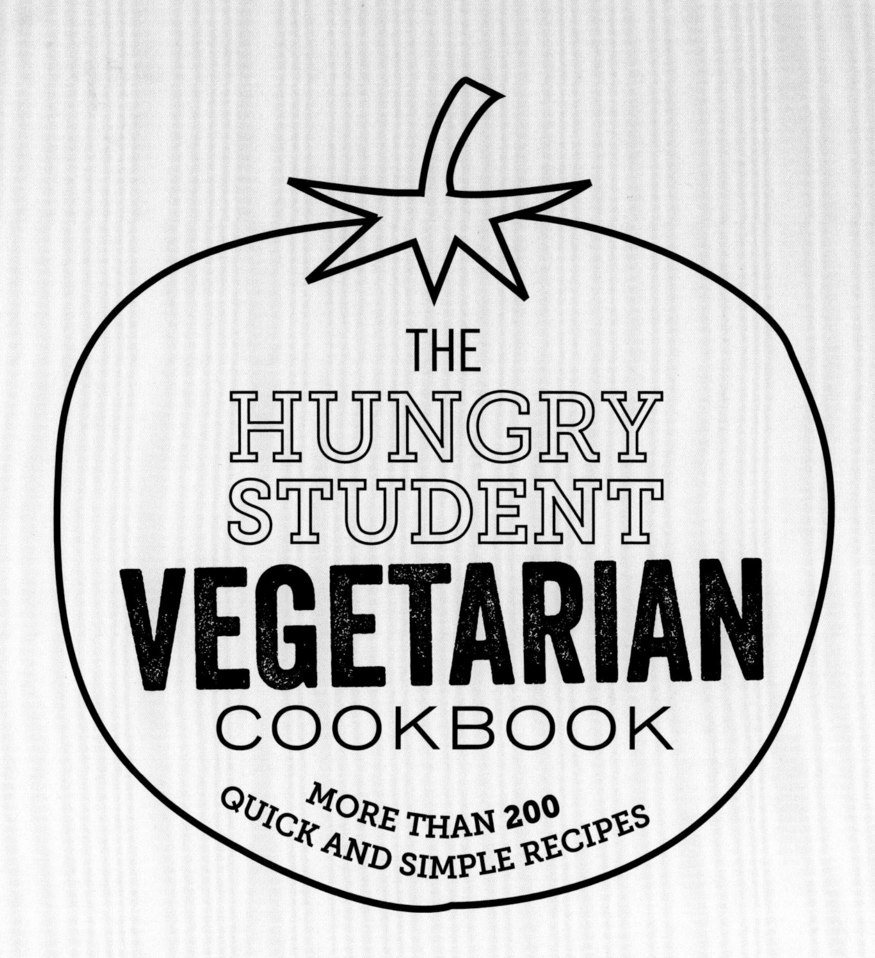
THE
HUNGRY
STUDENT
VEGETARIAN
COOKBOOK
MORE THAN 200
QUICK AND SIMPLE RECIPES

spruce

An Hachette UK Company
www.hachette.co.uk

First published in Great Britain in 2015 by
Spruce, a division of Octopus Publishing Group Ltd
Carmelite House, 50 Victoria Embankment
London EC4Y 0DZ
www.octopusbooks.co.uk

ISBN 978-1-84601-497-0

A CIP catalogue record for this book is available from the British Library

Printed and bound in China
10 9 8 7 6 5

Drinking excessive alcohol can significantly damage your health. The UK Health Department recommends men do not regularly exceed 3–4 units a day and women 2–3 units. Never operate a vehicle when you have been drinking alcohol. Octopus Publishing Group accepts no liability or responsibility for any consequences resulting from the use of or reliance upon the information contained herein.

This book includes dishes made with nuts and nut derivatives. Do not mix metric and imperial measurements. Standard level spoon measurements are used throughout.
1 tablespoon = one 15 ml spoon
1 teaspoon = one 5 ml spoon

Ovens should be preheated to the specified temperature — if using a fan-assisted oven, follow the manufacturer's instructions for adjusting the time and the temperature

Contents

Introduction 4

Bring on Brekky 8

Comfort Food 24

Roasted & Baked 58

Made in a Flash 106

All the Carbs 142

Salads, Sides & Snacks 184

What's for Afters? 208

Bar, Drinks & Basics 234

Index 252

Acknowledgements 256

INTRODUCTION

Leaving home is both an exciting and daunting prospect. Although you probably feel ready to move out and gain your independence, there's a lot to be said for clothes that miraculously get washed and ironed, a fridge full of fresh food and plates that don't require week-old takeaway to be chiselled off before they can be used. And then there's the big issue of cooking for yourself; something you will have to master quickly unless you are resigned to three years of cereal and toast.

If kitchen appliances and cooking techniques are alien concepts, don't worry – a few key skills and a handful of go-to recipes are all you need to ensure you don't die of boredom at mealtimes. Even the most inexperienced cook can learn how to rustle up a quick pasta dinner or do something creative with eggs. If nothing else, necessity will generally help you to overcome any kitchen phobias – if no one else is going to cook your dinner, you'll have to roll up your sleeves and cook it yourself.

BUDGETING

It might be dull but good budgeting will get you through college without going into serious debt. When it comes to food, you'll discover that you can actually enjoy a more varied and healthy diet by shopping sensibly and cooking your own meals, than by handing your weekly food allowance over the counter at a fast-food outlet or convenience store.

If you're living with friends you can save a fortune by organizing a communal food budget. It means you can take advantage of bulk-buy deals and food that's coming close to its sell-by date and being sold at a discount. A household budget also means you can take it in turns to do the weekly shop and to prepare meals, so you can all enjoy home-cooked food every night without having to spend too much time in the kitchen. If you're really organized, you could work out a weekly meal plan and shopping list, which will save time and money when you visit the supermarket.

When you're working out a budget, you need to take your total weekly living allowance into account. Deduct set expenditure such as rent, utility bills and travel expenses, then the amount you're left with can be divided between your shopping basket and the pub.

If you are a vegetarian in a meat-eating household, you will need to make sure you include a good variety of beans, veggies and pulses on the shopping list if it's not your turn to visit the supermarket – carnivores might automatically head for the meat aisles for their protein fix and could need a nudge to push the trolley over to pulses.

SHARING

If you come from a big family, you should be used to sharing but this probably doesn't extend to food. The first time your special block of cheese or slice of chocolate cake mysteriously disappears from the fridge may well come as a shock but this is something you need to get used to. No matter how close you are to your housemates, there will come a time when drunken munchies or hungover desperation will lead them to help themselves to whatever culinary treats are to hand.

It makes sense to put a few house rules in place when you first move in. If you're shopping as a household you need to be clear about whether this is for the ingredients for all your meals, or just household basics like bread and milk. If anyone wants something additional, they should pay for it themselves – but that also means it's out of bounds. Obviously, there are going to be a few blurred lines if you have one communal fridge and the kitchen cupboards are a household free-for-all. Again, you need to decide if you going to have some individual space for your own food, or whether you trust everyone to stick to the rules and keep their hands off the exotic fruit platter that you've been looking forward to eating all day.

Milk, bread and other essentials will need to be topped up more often than the weekly shop so it's a good idea to have a separate kitty for this, and take it in turns to buy it. You could all put a few pounds a week into a pot to cover the cost and any leftover money can be added to the food budget to buy a few treats.

STAY HEALTHY

Kitchens are breeding grounds for a number of nasty bugs and the combination of living in close proximity to other people, and the student aversion to washing up, means you're more likely to fall prey to them. It only takes a few minutes a day to wipe kitchen surfaces with antibacterial spray and, if the luxury of a dishwasher has evaded you, the same goes for washing up. A cleaning rota can help to solve the problem of certain people dodging their housekeeping duties. Put it somewhere prominent so the culprits can be named and shamed but also make it realistic – if some people have a fear of mopping floors but are unfazed by dusting, then allocate tasks among your housemates accordingly.

A clean kitchen will definitely lower your chances of a stopover in hospital but you also need to take care when handling and preparing food. Vegetarians have a natural advantage here, as many cases of food poisoning and other food-related illnesses are linked to raw meat contaminating other foods, or not cooking meat properly. However, you're not completely off the hook.

- **COVER UP** Uncovered food will attract flies – always keep food covered or stored in the fridge. The same goes for bins: empty them once they're full; don't try and squeeze more rubbish in.
- **FRUIT BATH** Always thoroughly rinse fruit and vegetables before you eat or cook with them. You don't know how many other people have handled them before they reached your kitchen.
- **FURRY FRIENDS** Mice love spilt food, overflowing food bins and leftovers on display. The problem is, so do a lot of students...
- **STRANGE SMELLS** If an ingredient smells dodgy, chances are it's off and shouldn't be eaten. And if you do pick up a bargain at the supermarket on its use-by date, stick to the advice and eat it that day.

KITCHEN EQUIPMENT

You need to accept that your kitchen won't be decked out like a showroom and you will probably have to make do with limited storage and preparation space. You will also be relying on donations of kitchen equipment from your family, or bargain-basement sets of crockery and pans.

However, you don't need to be kitted out like a celebrity chef to create quality meals. Choose your implements wisely and – as long as the oven works – you'll be able to put together the recipes in this book with the minimum equipment. Here are some basics you'll need to get you started.

Utensils – Measuring jug, two different-sized mixing bowls, wooden spoon, rolling pin, grater, spatula, chopping board, vegetable peeler, whisk, colander, sharp knives (one small for prepping veg and one large for chopping, slicing bread etc).

Pots and pans – Large and small saucepan (with lids), large nonstick frying pan, steamer (useful but a metal colander over a pan will work fine). A wok is handy but not essential.

Cookware – Baking sheet, roasting tin, flameproof casserole dish, large rectangular ovenproof dish (for lasagnes, bakes etc), wire cooling rack, cake tins, muffin tin and pastry cutters (if you're a baker).

A stick blender is ideal for blending soups or making smoothies, but if there's a spare food processor hanging around in a cupboard at the family home, this would be a good addition to your kitchen. They're great for chopping large quantities of vegetables, making sauces, and cakes. If you want to make fresh juice and don't have a juicer, they can also be used to juice fresh fruit.

Obviously, if you have a particular penchant for Spanish food or homemade bread, you'll probably want to pack a paella dish or your collection of loaf tins in your suitcase. There's an almost endless list of kitchen implements and gadgets for every possible ingredient and preparation technique. But as long as you have the basics, you'll eat well.

If you know your housemates, it's a good idea to make a list of everything you're going to need and then divide it up. There's no point moving in and discovering that all four of you have brought citrus parers but you don't have a saucepan between you. The same goes for crockery – you don't all need to bring a full set of plates, bowls and cups. Apart from taking up huge amounts of valuable kitchen space, the more crockery there is to use, the less washing up will get done.

ESSENTIAL INGREDIENTS

Whether you turn up on your first day with armfuls of food or you sit down with your housemates and plan your first week's shopping, there are certain ingredients that you'll use time and again and you'll need to keep in the storecupboard.

Condiments – Salt and pepper are the mainstays of many recipes and good seasoning will lift an ordinary dish up to the next dimension. You will also need vegetable oil for cooking and olive oil for dressings and sauces. Vegetable bouillon powder or stock cubes are another mainstay, but you can also make your own stock from scratch (see page 246). Ketchup, mayonnaise and mustard should also be present in any student kitchen.

Butter – Toast is a student staple so a good supply of butter or margarine is essential. This is also an important ingredient for mash.

Spices – You don't need a huge variety of spices but a few essentials like curry powder, cumin seeds, paprika or turmeric will add depth and heat to dishes. If using curry pastes, check the labels to make sure they are suitable for vegetarians.

Onions and garlic – From Indian curries to Italian pasta dishes, these two ingredients are essential to the success of so many dishes – always keep a ready supply.

Dried pasta and rice – Both have a long shelf life, are extremely versatile and provide you with a good source of carbohydrates. Don't go too crazy with the pasta shapes – stick to a couple of favourites – and choose wholemeal for a healthier option.

Cans – Cans of beans (kidney beans and butter beans, as well as the baked variety), sweetcorn, chickpeas and chopped tomatoes are great storecupboard staples when the budget is tight. They are cheap and can be used to bulk up soups, stews and casseroles or added to veggie curries and salads.

Freezer staples – Depending on space, it's a good idea to keep a spare loaf of bread tucked away for emergency breakfasts. A few bags of frozen vegetables could also get you out of a tight spot, while gluts of seasonal fruit like blackberries or raspberries can be frozen and used in smoothies and desserts.

GETTING STARTED

With a bit of patience and practice you will soon be enjoying delicious home-cooked meals that don't cost a fortune, and in the following pages you'll find everything you need to guide you through your culinary adventures at college.

BUDGETING

Boring as it may be, unless you want to spend the last month of each term hiding in your hovel and eating plain rice, budgeting is a necessary part of student life. Each recipe in this book is rated from 1 to 3, with 1s providing end-of-term saviours that can be scraped together for a pittance, and 3s to splash out and impress all your friends.

Bring on Brekky

POTATO RÖSTI WITH FRAZZLED EGGS

BUCKWHEAT PANCAKES

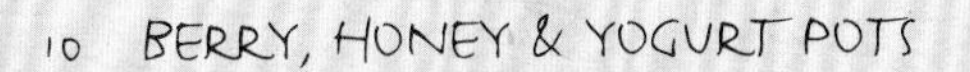

10 BERRY, HONEY & YOGURT POTS

12 PUMPKIN SEED & APRICOT MUESLI

13 HONEY-ROASTED GRANOLA

14 QUINOA PORRIDGE WITH RASPBERRIES

16 BLUEBERRY & LEMON PANCAKES

17 BUCKWHEAT PANCAKES

18 TOMATO, PEPPER & EGG TORTILLAS

19 PESTO SCRAMBLED EGGS

22 POTATO RÖSTI WITH FRAZZLED EGGS

23 OVEN-BAKED SAUSAGE BRUNCH

BLUEBERRY & LEMON PANCAKES

PESTO SCRAMBLED EGGS

HONEY-ROASTED GRANOLA

Berry, HONEY & YOGURT Pots

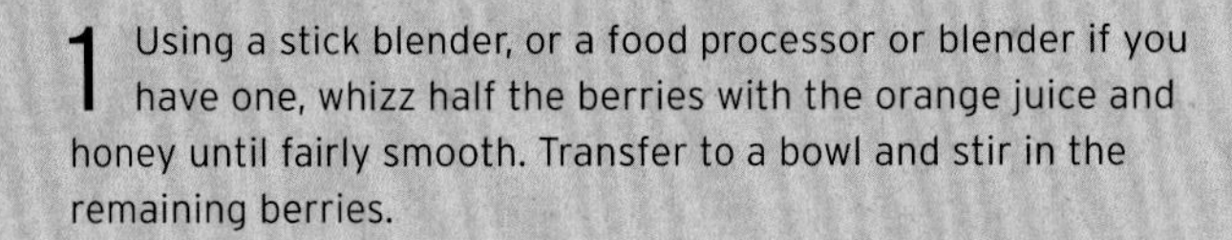

1 Using a stick blender, or a food processor or blender if you have one, whizz half the berries with the orange juice and honey until fairly smooth. Transfer to a bowl and stir in the remaining berries.

2 Divide one-third of the berry mixture between four glasses or small bowls. Top with half the yogurt. Layer with half the remaining berry mixture and top with the remaining yogurt.

3 Top with the remaining berry mixture and sprinkle over the granola just before serving.

400 g (13 oz) frozen mixed berries (thawed)
juice of 1 orange
6 tablespoons clear honey
400 ml (14 fl oz) vanilla yogurt
50 g (2 oz) granola

Serves **4**
Prep time **10 minutes**

PUMPKIN SEED & APRICOT MUESLI

IF YOU'RE NOT A MORNING PERSON, MAKE THIS MUESLI THE NIGHT BEFORE. CARRY OUT STEP 1 AND PUT THE MIXTURE IN THE FRIDGE OVERNIGHT. THE NEXT MORNING, ADD THE APPLES AND MILK. THIS WILL ALSO GIVE A SOFTER-TEXTURED MUESLI.

50 g (2 oz) rolled jumbo oats
1 tablespoon sultanas or raisins
1 tablespoon pumpkin or sunflower seeds
1 tablespoon chopped almonds
25 g (1 oz) ready-to-eat dried apricots, chopped
2 tablespoons orange or apple juice
2 small dessert apples, peeled and grated
3 tablespoons soya milk or milk

Serves **2**
Prep time **10 minutes**

AFFORDABILITY 1

1 Place the oats, sultanas or raisins, seeds, almonds and apricots in a bowl with the fruit juice.

2 Add the grated apples and stir to mix. Top with your chosen milk and serve.

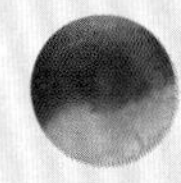

STUDENT TIP

Take a calculator to the supermarket (or use your Smartphone). Adding up prices as you add food to the trolley is a good way to shop within your budget and make informed choices about what you buy.

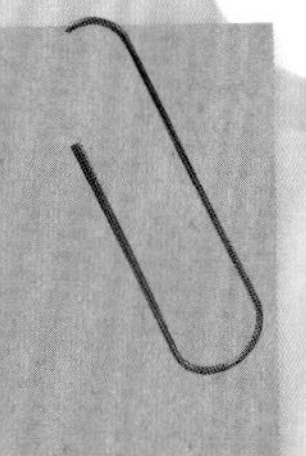

HONEY-ROASTED GRANOLA

5 tablespoons clear honey
2 tablespoons vegetable oil
250 g (8 oz) porridge oats
50 g (2 oz) hazelnuts, roughly chopped
50 g (2 oz) blanched almonds, roughly chopped
50 g (2 oz) dried cranberries
50 g (2 oz) dried blueberries

To serve
milk or yogurt
fresh fruit (optional)

Serves **4**
Prep time **10 minutes, plus cooling**
Cooking time **25–30 minutes**

1 Heat the honey and oil together gently in a small saucepan. Mix the oats and nuts together thoroughly in a large bowl. Pour over the warm honey mixture and stir well to combine.

2 Spread the mixture over a large nonstick baking sheet and bake in a preheated oven, 150°C (300°F), Gas Mark 2, for 20–25 minutes, stirring once, until golden.

3 Leave the granola to cool, then stir in the dried berries. Serve with milk or yogurt and fresh fruit, if liked. Any remaining granola can be stored in an airtight container.

Quinoa Porridge WITH RASPBERRIES

600 ml (1 pint) milk
100 g (3½ oz) quinoa
2 tablespoons caster sugar
½ teaspoon ground cinnamon
125 g (4 oz) fresh raspberries
2 tablespoons mixed seeds, such as sunflower, linseed, pumpkin and hemp
2 tablespoons clear honey

Serves **2**
Prep time **5 minutes**
Cooking time **25-30 minutes**

1 Bring the milk to the boil in a small saucepan, add the quinoa and return to the boil. Reduce the heat to low, cover with a lid and simmer for about 15 minutes until three-quarters of the milk has been absorbed.

2 Stir the sugar and cinnamon into the pan, re-cover and cook for 8–10 minutes or until almost all the milk has been absorbed and the quinoa is tender.

3 Spoon the porridge into bowls, then top with the raspberries, sprinkle over the seeds and drizzle with the honey. Serve immediately.

BLUEBERRY & LEMON *Pancakes*

125 g (4 oz) self-raising flour
1 teaspoon baking powder
finely grated rind of ½ lemon
1 tablespoon caster sugar
1 egg, lightly beaten
1 tablespoon lemon juice
150 ml (¼ pint) semi-skimmed milk
125 g (4 oz) blueberries
vegetable oil, for frying

To serve
butter
jam

Serves **4**
Prep time **10 minutes**
Cooking time **20 minutes**

1 Sift the flour and baking powder into a bowl and stir in the lemon rind and sugar. Add the egg and lemon juice and gradually whisk in the milk to make a smooth, thick batter. Stir in the blueberries.

2 Heat a large nonstick frying pan and rub it with a piece of kitchen paper drizzled with a little oil. Drop spoonfuls of the mixture, spaced well apart, in the pan and cook for 2–3 minutes until bubbles form on the surface and the underside is golden brown, then turn the pancakes over and cook on the other side. Wrap in a clean tea towel and keep warm while cooking the remaining mixture in the same way.

AFFORDABILITY 1

BUCKWHEAT PANCAKES

1 Sift the flours into a bowl and add the grains left in the sieve. Beat the egg and milk together in a jug, then slowly add to the flour. Stir until a smooth batter forms. If the mixture is a little thick, add a little more milk. Leave to stand for 20 minutes, then stir again.

2 Put 1 teaspoon of the oil in a nonstick frying pan. When it's hot, add 2 tablespoons of the pancake mixture and shake the pan so it spreads. Cook for 2 minutes until the underside is lightly browned, then turn the pancake over and cook on the other side for a minute or so. Transfer to a plate and keep warm in a low oven while cooking the remaining mixture in the same way.

50 g (2 oz) wholemeal flour
50 g (2 oz) buckwheat flour
1 egg
300 ml (½ pint) skimmed milk
8 teaspoons olive oil

To serve
fresh fruit
natural yogurt

Serves **4**
Prep time **5 minutes, plus standing**
Cooking time **25 minutes**

Tomato, Pepper & Egg TORTILLAS

1 tablespoon vegetable oil
1 small onion, finely chopped
1 garlic clove, crushed
1 mild green chilli, deseeded and finely chopped
1 small green pepper, cored, deseeded and thinly sliced
1 small red pepper, cored, deseeded and thinly sliced
400 g (13 oz) can chopped tomatoes
2 tablespoons tomato ketchup
4 eggs
4 corn tortillas
smoked paprika, for sprinkling
salt and pepper

Serves **4**
Prep time **15 minutes**
Cooking time **25–30 minutes**

1 Heat the oil in a large frying pan with a lid, add the onion, garlic, chilli and peppers and cook over a medium heat for about 10–15 minutes, stirring frequently, until the peppers are soft. Stir in the tomatoes and ketchup and season with salt and pepper. Bring to the boil, then reduce the heat and simmer for 5 minutes until thickened.

2 Make four shallow hollows in the tomato mixture with the back of a spoon and break an egg into each hollow. Cover the pan and cook over a low heat for about 5 minutes until just set.

3 Meanwhile, warm the tortillas according to the pack instructions. Place a tortilla on each warmed serving plate and carefully transfer the egg and tomato mixture on to each tortilla. Serve immediately, sprinkled with a little smoked paprika.

Pesto SCRAMBLED EGGS

12 eggs
100 ml (3½ fl oz) single cream
  or milk
25 g (1 oz) butter
4 slices of granary
  bread, toasted
4 tablespoons homemade
  (see page 249) or ready-
  made pesto
salt and pepper

Serves **4**
Prep time **5 minutes**
Cooking time **5 minutes**

1 Beat the eggs, cream or milk and a little salt and pepper together in a bowl. Melt the butter in a large nonstick frying pan, add the egg mixture and stir over a low heat with a wooden spoon until cooked to your liking.

2 Put a slice of toast on each warmed serving plate. Spoon a quarter of the scrambled eggs on to each slice of toast, make a small indent in the centre and add a tablespoonful of pesto. Serve immediately.

SHOPPING ON A BUDGET

When you're on a tight budget, food can often get pushed down the list of priorities. With studying, sleeping and partying taking up the majority of your time, it can be tricky to find any extra hours in the day to shop around for good-value, good-quality food. However, it's worth spending a bit of time sniffing out some culinary bargains – you'll save money and also add more variety to your diet.

ONLINE CHECKOUT

Shopping online is a good way to stick rigidly to a shopping list, as the bright lights and branding of the supermarket are safely out of reach. You can see exactly how much you're spending as you fill your basket and quickly delete items if you need to rein in your budget before you check out. While most supermarkets charge for delivery, it could still work out cheaper than getting the bus or paying for parking, and you'll often find that daytime slots cost less, which is perfect for students.

MARKETS

While it's true that many of the gourmet delights on offer at local farmers' markets might be beyond your limited means, seasonal fruit and vegetables can work out a lot cheaper. High-street markets are also a good source of edible bargains, and if you can hold out until the end of the day, you will usually get even more for your money, as stallholders try to sell off produce with a shorter shelf life.

POOLING RESOURCES

For certain foods, it works out cheaper to buy in bulk so it might be worth setting up a weekly food budget with your housemates and shopping together. Long-life ingredients such as pasta, rice, breakfast cereals, cans and cartons are all cheaper in larger quantities so it makes sense to stock up your storecupboards and take advantage of supermarket deals. If you're really organized, you could also work out a cooking rota, which means everyone can enjoy home-cooked meals without having to cook every night.

MENU PLANNER

Don't worry, this doesn't have to be a sophisticated, interactive spreadsheet; a few ideas jotted down on a notepad will do the trick. It's common knowledge that if you shop for meals, you'll spend less and waste less than if you wander the aisles picking up random ingredients with no recipes in mind.

POTATO RÖSTI WITH FRAZZLED EGGS

750 g (1½ lb) Desiree potatoes, peeled
1 onion, thinly sliced
2 teaspoons chopped rosemary
4 tablespoons vegetable oil
4 large eggs
salt and pepper
chopped parsley, to garnish

Serves **4**
Prep time **15 minutes**
Cooking time **15 minutes**

1 Using a grater, coarsely grate the potatoes. Wrap in a clean tea towel and squeeze out the excess liquid over the sink. Transfer to a bowl and stir in the onion, rosemary and salt and pepper.

2 Heat half the oil in a large frying pan. Divide the potato mixture into quarters and spoon into four 12 cm (5 inch) mounds in the pan, pressing down to form patties. Cook over a medium heat for 5 minutes on each side until cooked through, then transfer to warmed serving plates and keep warm in a moderate oven.

3 Heat the remaining oil in the frying pan for about 1 minute until very hot, add the eggs, two at a time, and fry until the whites are bubbly and crisp. Serve the eggs on the rösti, garnished with chopped parsley.

OVEN-BAKED Sausage Brunch

1 tablespoon vegetable oil
4 vegetarian sausages
2 potatoes, scrubbed and cut into 1 cm (½ inch) cubes
4 mini portobello mushrooms, trimmed
2 tomatoes, halved
2 large eggs
pepper

Serves **2**
Prep time **10 minutes**
Cooking time **30 minutes**

1 Heat the oil in a nonstick ovenproof dish or roasting dish in a preheated oven, 200°C (400°F), Gas Mark 6, until hot.

2 Add the sausages and potatoes to the hot oil and turn to coat in the oil. Cook in the oven for 10 minutes.

3 Remove the dish from the oven, add the mushrooms and tomatoes and turn with the sausages and potatoes to coat in the oil. Return to the oven and cook for a further 10–12 minutes until the potatoes are golden and the sausages are cooked through.

4 Make two separate spaces in the baked mixture and break an egg into each. Return to the oven and cook for a further 3–4 minutes until the eggs are softly set. Grind over some black pepper and serve immediately.

26 HEARTY MINESTRONE
27 CURRIED PARSNIP SOUP
28 BUTTER BEAN & VEGETABLE SOUP
29 SPICY LENTIL & TOMATO SOUP
30 GREEN LENTIL SOUP WITH SPICED BUTTER
31 NEW POTATO, CORIANDER & LEEK SOUP
32 LEMON & SPINACH SOUP
34 LENTIL DHAL WITH POTATO CHAPATIS
35 TEMPEH BALTI
36 MASSAMAN VEGETABLE CURRY
37 POTATO, CAULIFLOWER & SPINACH CURRY
38 CHICKPEA PURÉE WITH EGGS & SPICED OIL
40 RED BEANS WITH COCONUT & CASHEWS
41 OKRA & COCONUT STEW
42 CHICKPEA & AUBERGINE TAGINE
44 TOMATO & CHICKPEA STEW
45 BEER & BARLEY STEW WITH DUMPLINGS
46 GOULASH WITH CHIVE DUMPLINGS
47 LENTIL & PARSNIP COTTAGE PIE
48 LENTIL BOLOGNESE
52 BUTTERED CAULIFLOWER CRUMBLE
53 ROMANESCO CAULIFLOWER CHEESE
54 GARDENER'S PIE
56 GNOCCHI WITH SAGE BUTTER
57 POTATO & ONION PIZZA

GARDENERS' PIE

Comfort Food

TOMATO & CHICKPEA STEW

POTATO & ONION PIZZA

LEMON & SPINACH SOUP

V

HEARTY *Minestrone*

3 carrots, roughly chopped
1 red onion, roughly chopped
6 celery sticks, roughly chopped
2 tablespoons vegetable oil
2 garlic cloves, crushed
200 g (7 oz) potatoes, peeled and cut into 1 cm (½ inch) dice
4 tablespoons tomato purée
1.5 litres (2½ pints) Vegetable Stock (see page 246)
400 g (13 oz) can chopped tomatoes
150 g (5 oz) short-shaped soup pasta
400 g (13 oz) can cannellini beans, drained
100 g (3 ½ oz) baby spinach leaves
salt and pepper
crusty bread, to serve

Serves 4
Prep time **15 minutes**
Cooking time **15-20 minutes**

1 Finely chop the carrots, onion and celery. (You can do this in a food processor, if you have one.)

2 Heat the oil in a large saucepan, add the chopped vegetables, garlic, potatoes, tomato purée, stock, tomatoes and pasta. Bring to the boil, then reduce the heat, cover with a lid and simmer for 12–15 minutes.

3 Tip in the cannellini beans and the spinach for the final 2 minutes of cooking time. Season to taste and serve with crusty bread.

CURRIED Parsnip Soup

1 Heat the butter and oil in a large saucepan, add the onion, garlic and ginger and cook over a medium heat for 4–5 minutes until softened. Stir in the curry powder and cumin seeds and cook, stirring, for 2 minutes, then stir in the parsnips, making sure that they are well coated in the spice mixture.

2 Pour over the stock and bring to the boil, then reduce the heat, cover with a lid and simmer for 20–25 minutes until the parsnips are tender. Season to taste with salt and pepper.

3 Blend the soup with a stick blender until smooth, or transfer to a food processor or blender, in batches, to blend. Reheat gently if necessary.

4 Ladle into warmed cups, add dollops of yogurt and garnish with the coriander. Serve with warmed naan bread.

25 g (1 oz) butter
1 tablespoon vegetable oil
1 onion, chopped
2 garlic cloves, crushed
2.5 cm (1 inch) piece of fresh root ginger, peeled and chopped
1 tablespoon medium curry powder
1 teaspoon cumin seeds
750 g (1½ lb) parsnips, peeled and chopped
1 litre (1¾ pints) Vegetable Stock (see page 246)
salt and pepper

To serve
natural yogurt
2 tablespoons chopped fresh coriander
naan bread

Serves **4**
Prep time **15 minutes**
Cooking time **30–35 minutes**

AFFORDABILITY 1

Butter Bean & VEGETABLE SOUP

1 tablespoon vegetable oil
2 teaspoons smoked paprika
1 celery stick, sliced
2 carrots, sliced
1 leek, trimmed and sliced
600 ml (1 pint) Vegetable Stock (see page 246)
400 g (13 oz) can chopped tomatoes
400 g (13 oz) can butter beans, rinsed and drained
2 teaspoons chopped rosemary
salt and pepper
50 g (2 oz) Parmesan-style cheese, grated, to serve

Serves **4**
Prep time **10 minutes**
Cooking time **25 minutes**

1 Heat the oil in a large saucepan, add the paprika, celery, carrots and leek and cook over a medium heat for 3–4 minutes until the vegetables are slightly softened.

2 Pour over the stock and tomatoes and add the butter beans and rosemary. Season to taste with salt and pepper and bring to the boil, then reduce the heat, cover with a lid and simmer for 15 minutes or until the vegetables are just tender.

3 Ladle into warmed bowls and sprinkle with the cheese and freshly ground black pepper.

STUDENT TIP
Don't fall for the trap of buying packaged fruit and vegetables. You can save money simply by filling up a bag with loose produce. Next time you go to the supermarket, compare the price per kg of packaged and loose vegetables – you'll never buy plastic-wrapped carrots again.

SPICY LENTIL & Tomato Soup

V

250 g (8 oz) red lentils
1 tablespoon vegetable oil
1 large onion, finely chopped
1 garlic clove, finely chopped
1 celery stick, finely chopped
200 g (7 oz) canned chopped tomatoes
½ small green chilli, deseeded and finely chopped (optional)
½ teaspoon paprika
½ teaspoon harissa paste
½ teaspoon ground cumin
600 ml (1 pint) Vegetable Stock (see page 246) or water
salt and pepper
1 tablespoon chopped fresh coriander, to garnish

Serves 4
Prep time 10 minutes
Cooking time 40-50 minutes

1 Place the lentils in a bowl of water. Heat the oil in a large saucepan, add the onion, garlic and celery and fry over a low heat until softened.

2 Drain the lentils and add them to the vegetables with the tomatoes. Mix well. Add the chilli, if using, paprika, harissa paste, cumin and stock or water and season with salt and pepper. Cover with a lid and simmer gently for about 30–40 minutes until the lentils are soft, adding a little more stock or water if the soup gets too thick.

3 Ladle into warmed bowls and serve garnished with a little chopped coriander.

GREEN LENTIL SOUP

With Spiced Butter

SERVE THE SPICY BUTTER SEPARATELY FOR STIRRING INTO THE SOUP, SO THAT EACH PERSON CAN 'HOT UP' THEIR OWN PORTION ACCORDING TO PERSONAL TASTE.

1 Heat the oil in a saucepan, add the onions and fry for 3 minutes. Add the bay leaves, lentils, stock and turmeric. Bring to the boil, then reduce the heat, cover with a lid and simmer for 20 minutes until the lentils are tender and turning mushy.

2 Meanwhile, to prepare the spiced butter, beat the butter with the garlic, paprika, cumin seeds and chilli and transfer to a small serving dish.

3 Stir the coriander into the soup, remove the bay leaves and season to taste with salt and pepper. Serve with the spiced butter in a separate bowl for stirring into the soup.

3 tablespoons vegetable oil
2 onions, sliced
2 bay leaves
175 g (6 oz) green lentils, rinsed
1 litre (1¾ pints) Vegetable Stock (see page 246)
½ teaspoon turmeric
small handful of coriander leaves, roughly chopped
salt and pepper

Spiced butter
50 g (2 oz) lightly salted butter, softened
1 large garlic clove, crushed
1 teaspoon paprika
1 teaspoon cumin seeds
1 red chilli, deseeded and thinly sliced

Serves **4**
Prep time **10 minutes**
Cooking time **25 minutes**

NEW POTATO, *Coriander* & LEEK SOUP

1 Halve each potato, or cut into 1 cm (3/4 inch) slices if large. Halve the leeks lengthways, then cut across into thin shreds.

2 Melt the butter in a heavy-based saucepan, add the mustard seeds, onion, garlic and potatoes and fry gently for 5 minutes. Add the stock and nutmeg and bring just to the boil. Reduce the heat, cover with a lid and simmer gently for about 10 minutes until the potatoes are just tender.

3 Stir in the leeks and coriander and cook for a further 5 minutes. Season to taste with salt and pepper and serve with warm bread.

500 g (1 lb) waxy new potatoes, such as Jersey Royals, scrubbed
3 small leeks, trimmed
40 g (1½ oz) butter
1 tablespoon black mustard seeds
1 onion, chopped
1 garlic clove, thinly sliced
1 litre (1 3/4 pints) Vegetable Stock (see page 246)
plenty of grated nutmeg
small handful of fresh coriander, roughly chopped
salt and pepper
warm bread, to serve

Serves **4**
Prep time **10 minutes**
Cooking time **20 minutes**

Lemon & SPINACH SOUP

2 tablespoons vegetable oil
1 large onion, finely chopped
2 garlic cloves, finely chopped
175 g (6 oz) long grain white rice, rinsed
1.2 litres (2 pints) Vegetable Stock (see page 246)
4 tablespoons lemon juice
3 large eggs, beaten
200 g (7 oz) spinach leaves, tough stalks removed, chopped
salt and pepper
2 tablespoons chopped parsley, to garnish
2 tablespoons grated Parmesan-style cheese, to serve

Serves 4
Prep time 10 minutes
Cooking time 25-30 minutes

1 Heat the oil in a large saucepan or casserole, add the onion and garlic and cook gently for 7–8 minutes until softened. Stir in the rice and cook for 1 minute, then pour in the stock. Simmer gently for 12–15 minutes until the rice is just tender. Remove from the heat.

2 In a small bowl, whisk the lemon juice with the beaten eggs and a pinch of salt. Continue whisking while you add a ladleful of the hot soup in a slow, steady stream, then whisk the egg mixture into the saucepan of soup.

3 Return the pan to a very low heat, and continue stirring for 2-3 minutes until the soup has thickened slightly, taking care not to allow it to boil. Stir in the chopped spinach and season to taste, then ladle into warmed bowls and scatter with the chopped parsley. Serve with the grated cheese.

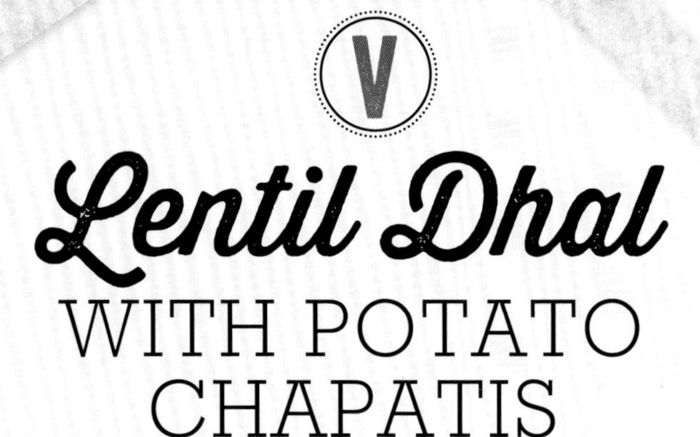

Lentil Dhal WITH POTATO CHAPATIS

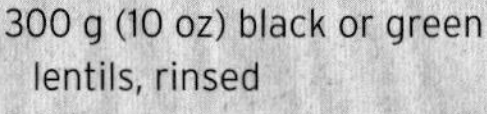

300 g (10 oz) black or green lentils, rinsed
2 tablespoons vegetable oil
1 onion, chopped
2 garlic cloves, finely chopped
2 tablespoons mild curry paste (suitable for vegetarians)
300 ml (½ pint) Vegetable Stock (see page 246)
2 tomatoes, roughly chopped
3 tablespoons chopped fresh coriander
1 tablespoon lemon or lime juice
salt and pepper

Chapatis
500 g (1 lb) potatoes, peeled and cut into chunks
50 g (2 oz) plain flour or spelt flour, plus extra for dusting
2 teaspoons ground cumin
1 teaspoon turmeric
vegetable oil, for frying

Serves **4**
Prep time **30 minutes, plus cooling**
Cooking time **1 hour**

1 Cook the potatoes in a saucepan of salted boiling water for 12–15 minutes until tender. Drain, return to the saucepan and mash until smooth. Tip into a bowl and leave to cool.

2 Tip the lentils into a saucepan, cover with boiling water and cook for 15 minutes to soften. Drain.

3 Heat the oil in a saucepan, add the onion and fry for 5 minutes. Add the garlic and curry paste, stirring to mix. Add the stock, tomatoes and lentils, cover with a lid and cook for 15–20 minutes until thick and pulpy.

4 Meanwhile, beat the flour, spices and a little pepper into the potatoes to make a smooth soft dough. Turn out on to a floured surface and divide into eight pieces. Roll out each on a lightly floured surface until about 12 cm (5 inches) in diameter.

5 Put 1 teaspoon oil in a frying pan, tilting the pan so the oil coats the base. Add a chapati and cook for 1–2 minutes on each side until lightly browned. Transfer to a plate and keep warm while cooking the remainder in the same way, adding a dash more oil if the pan runs dry. Stir the coriander and lemon or lime juice into the dhal and serve with the chapatis.

TEMPEH BALTI

V

250 g (8 oz) tempeh, cut into 1 cm (½ inch) cubes
3 garlic cloves, crushed
25 g (1 oz) fresh root ginger, peeled and grated
2 onions, roughly chopped
6 cardamom pods
2 teaspoons cumin seeds
2 teaspoons coriander seeds
3 tablespoons vegetable oil
2 cinnamon sticks
2 bay leaves
6 whole cloves
1 red chilli, deseeded and chopped
½ teaspoon turmeric
2 x 400 g (13 oz) cans chopped tomatoes
2 teaspoons caster sugar
500 g (1 lb) potatoes, cut into cubes
225 g (7½ oz) spinach leaves, tough stalks removed

Serves **4**
Prep time **20 minutes**
Cooking time **30 minutes**

1 Mix the tempeh in a bowl with the garlic and ginger. Using a stick blender, or a food processor or blender if you have one, whizz the onions and 2 tablespoons water to a purée.

2 Lightly crush the cardamom pods with the cumin and coriander with a pestle and mortar. Alternatively, put them in a plastic food bag and crush to a fine powder with the back of a spoon.

3 Heat the oil in a large nonstick saucepan and fry the crushed spices with the cinnamon, bay leaves and cloves for 30 seconds. Tip the onion purée into the pan and add the chilli and turmeric. Cook for 1 minute, then add the tomatoes, sugar and potatoes and cover with a lid. Simmer gently for 20 minutes until the potatoes are tender and the sauce is thick. Add the tempeh and cook for a further 5 minutes.

4 Add the spinach to the pan, stirring it into the sauce until it starts to wilt. Remove the bay leaves and cook for a further 2 minutes or until the spinach is soft and coated with the sauce. Serve immediately.

MASSAMAN VEGETABLE CURRY

V

2 tablespoons vegetable oil
2 onions, chopped
2 garlic cloves, crushed
2 tablespoons Massaman curry paste (suitable for vegetarians)
300 ml (½ pint) hot Vegetable Stock (see page 246)
400 ml (14 fl oz) can coconut milk
2 tablespoons light muscovado or caster sugar
625 g (1 ¼ lb) Charlotte or salad potatoes
200 g (7 oz) green beans, halved
25 g (1 oz) fresh coriander, chopped
salt and pepper

To serve
50 g (2 oz) roasted, unsalted peanuts, roughly chopped
boiled jasmine or long grain rice

Serves **3-4**
Prep time **15 minutes**
Cooking time **40 minutes**

1 Heat the oil in a large saucepan, add the onions and fry for 5 minutes until softened. Add the garlic and fry for a further 1 minute.

2 Blend in the curry paste, then the stock, coconut milk and sugar. Bring to the boil, reduce the heat to a gentle simmer and stir in the potatoes. Cover and cook gently for 25 minutes until the potatoes are very tender.

3 Add the green beans, cover with a lid and cook for a further 5 minutes until the beans have softened but retain a little crunch. Stir in the coriander and season to taste with salt and pepper. Spoon into warmed bowls with the rice and serve scattered with the peanuts.

POTATO, CAULIFLOWER & SPINACH *Curry*

V

3 tablespoons vegetable oil
450 g (14½ oz) potatoes, peeled and cut into bite-sized chunks
1 large onion, roughly chopped
4 tablespoons medium curry paste (suitable for vegetarians)
½ small cauliflower, about 250 g (8 oz), cut into chunky florets
300 ml (½ pint) Vegetable Stock (see page 246)
200 ml (7 fl oz) coconut milk
150 g (5 oz) frozen leaf spinach
chopped fresh coriander, to garnish (optional)
cooked rice or warm naan bread, to serve

Serves 4
Prep time 10 minutes
Cooking time 25-30 minutes

1 Heat the oil in a large saucepan, add the potatoes and onion and cook over a medium heat for 5-6 minutes, stirring occasionally, until the vegetables are tinged with colour and begin to soften. Stir in the curry paste and cook for 1 minute to cook the spices.

2 Tip the cauliflower into the pan and stir to coat before adding the stock and coconut milk. Bring to the boil, then reduce the heat, cover with a lid and simmer gently for about 15 minutes, stirring occasionally, until the potatoes and cauliflower are tender and the sauce has thickened.

3 Stir in the frozen spinach and cook for a further 2-3 minutes until the spinach has wilted and the curry is hot. Serve sprinkled with chopped coriander, if liked, with rice or warm naan.

Chickpea Purée
WITH EGGS & SPICED OIL

SMOOTH CHICKPEA PURÉE, TOPPED WITH FRIED EGGS AND SPICY OIL, MAKES A GREAT SNACK AT ANY TIME OF THE DAY. SERVE ANY LEFTOVER PURÉE JUST AS YOU WOULD HUMMUS, WITH WARM PITTA BREAD.

1 Using a stick blender, or a food processor or blender if you have one, whizz the chickpeas with the garlic, tahini, milk, 2 tablespoons of the oil, 3 teaspoons of the lemon juice and salt and pepper until smooth, scraping the mixture from around the sides of the bowl halfway through. Transfer to a small heavy-based saucepan and heat through gently for about 3 minutes while preparing the eggs.

2 Heat another tablespoon of the oil in a small frying pan and fry the eggs. Pile the chickpea purée on to serving plates and top each mound with an egg.

3 Add the remaining oil and spices to the pan and heat through gently for 1 minute. Season lightly with salt and pepper and stir in the remaining lemon juice. Pour over the eggs and serve garnished with coriander leaves.

400 g (13 oz) can chickpeas, rinsed and drained
3 garlic cloves, sliced
4 tablespoons tahini
4 tablespoons milk
5 tablespoons olive oil
4 teaspoons lemon juice
2 eggs
½ teaspoon each of cumin, coriander and fennel seeds, lightly crushed
1 teaspoon sesame seeds
¼ teaspoon dried chilli flakes
good pinch of turmeric
salt and pepper
coriander leaves, to garnish

Serves **2**
Prep time **5 minutes**
Cooking time **10 minutes**

AFFORDABILITY
1

RED BEANS WITH COCONUT & CASHEWS

V

1 Heat the oil in a large saucepan, add the onions and carrots and fry for 3 minutes. Add the garlic, pepper and bay leaves and fry for a further 5 minutes until the vegetables are soft and well browned.

2 Stir in the paprika, tomato purée, coconut milk, tomatoes, stock and beans and bring to the boil. Reduce the heat and simmer, uncovered, for 12 minutes until the vegetables are tender.

3 Stir in the cashew nuts and coriander and remove the bay leaves. Season to taste with salt and pepper and heat through for 2 minutes. Serve with rice.

3 tablespoons vegetable oil
2 onions, chopped
2 small carrots, thinly sliced
3 garlic cloves, crushed
1 red pepper, cored, deseeded and chopped
2 bay leaves
1 tablespoon paprika
3 tablespoons tomato purée
400 ml (14 fl oz) can coconut milk
200 g (7 oz) canned chopped tomatoes
150 ml (1/4 pint) Vegetable Stock (see page 246)
425 g (14 oz) can red kidney beans, rinsed and drained
100 g (3 1/2 oz) unsalted, shelled cashew nuts, toasted
small handful of fresh coriander, roughly chopped
salt and pepper
boiled black or white rice, to serve

Serves 4
Prep time **10 minutes**
Cooking time **25 minutes**

AFFORDABILITY 2

OKRA & COCONUT STEW

V

375 g (12 oz) okra
4 tablespoons vegetable oil
2 onions, chopped
2 green peppers, cored, deseeded and cut into chunks
3 celery sticks, thinly sliced
3 garlic cloves, crushed
4 teaspoons Cajun spice blend
½ teaspoon turmeric
300 ml (½ pint) Vegetable Stock (see page 246)
400 ml (14 fl oz) can coconut milk
200 g (7 oz) frozen sweetcorn
juice of 1 lime
4 tablespoons chopped fresh coriander
salt and pepper

Serves **3-4**
Prep time **15 minutes**
Cooking time **40 minutes**

1 Trim the stalk ends from the okra and cut the pods into 1.5 cm (¾ inch) lengths.

2 Heat 2 tablespoons of the oil in a large saucepan and fry the okra for 5 minutes. Lift out with a slotted spoon on to a plate.

3 Add the remaining oil to the pan and very gently fry the onions, peppers and celery for 10 minutes, stirring frequently, until softened but not browned. Add the garlic, spice blend and turmeric and cook for 1 minute.

4 Pour in the stock and coconut milk and bring to the boil. Reduce the heat, cover with a lid and cook gently for 10 minutes. Return the okra to the pan with the sweetcorn, lime juice and coriander and cook for a further 10 minutes. Season to taste with salt and pepper and serve.

CHICKPEA & AUBERGINE TAGINE

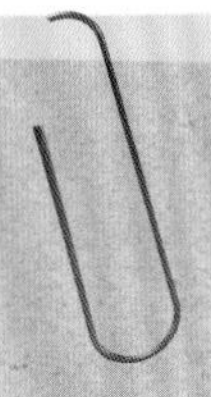

1 Heat the oil in a large saucepan, add the onion and garlic and cook over a medium heat for 4–5 minutes until softened. Stir in all the spices and cook, stirring, for 1 minute.

2 Add the aubergines and cook for about 5 minutes until starting to soften. Stir in all the remaining ingredients, except the parsley, and season to taste with salt and pepper.

3 Bring to the boil, then reduce the heat, cover with a lid and simmer for 30 minutes, stirring occasionally. Stir in the parsley, then serve with couscous.

1 tablespoon vegetable oil
1 large onion, sliced
2 garlic cloves, crushed
1 teaspoon ground cumin
1 teaspoon ground cinnamon
1 teaspoon turmeric
1 teaspoon paprika
2 aubergines, chopped into 3.5 cm (1½ inch) chunks
2 carrots, sliced
125 g (4 oz) soft dried pitted dates
400 g (13 oz) can chopped tomatoes
400 g (13 oz) can chickpeas, rinsed and drained
600 ml (1 pint) Vegetable Stock (see page 246)
4 slices of preserved lemon (optional)
2 tablespoons chopped flat leaf parsley
salt and pepper
couscous, to serve

Serves **4**
Prep time **10 minutes**
Cooking time **45 minutes**

COOKING TIP

Treat your freezer as your friend and cook double the portions so you can freeze half for another day. If you're taking the time to cook a tagine, lasagne, chilli or curry, it makes sense to prepare more, then freeze it in single portions.

V

TOMATO & CHICKPEA STEW

1 Heat the oil in a large, heavy-based saucepan, add the onion, pepper, garlic and ginger and cook for 6–7 minutes until softened.

2 Stir in the ground spices and cook for a further minute. Add the tomato purée, stock, tomato wedges and chickpeas, then cover with a lid and bring to the boil.

3 Season with salt and pepper, reduce the heat and simmer for about 8 minutes until thickened slightly and the tomatoes have softened. Serve garnished with the chopped parsley.

2½ tablespoons vegetable oil
1 large onion, chopped
1 green pepper, cored, deseeded and chopped
1 garlic clove, chopped
2.5 cm (1 inch) piece of fresh root ginger, peeled and chopped
1 teaspoon ground cumin
1 teaspoon ground coriander
2 tablespoons tomato purée
500 ml (17 fl oz) Vegetable Stock (see page 246)
4 large tomatoes, each cut into 8 wedges
2 x 400 g (13 oz) cans chickpeas, rinsed and drained
salt and pepper
2 tablespoons chopped flat leaf parsley, to garnish

Serves 4
Prep time 10 minutes
Cooking time 20 minutes

BEER & BARLEY STEW (V)

with dumplings

3 tablespoons vegetable oil
2 onions, roughly chopped
2 carrots, sliced
2 parsnips, sliced
1 leek, trimmed and sliced into rings
400 ml (14 fl oz) strong beer or ale
600 ml (1 pint) Vegetable Stock (see page 246)
100 g (3½ oz) pearl barley, rinsed
1 large potato, cut into 1 cm (½ inch) cubes
1 teaspoon dried thyme or mixed herbs
1–2 tablespoons grainy mustard
salt and pepper

Dumplings
150 g (5 oz) self-raising flour
75 g (3 oz) vegetable suet

Serves **4–5**
Prep time **20 minutes**
Cooking time **1 hour 20 minutes**

1 Heat the oil in a large saucepan or flameproof casserole, add the onions, carrots, parsnips and leeks and fry gently for 10–15 minutes, stirring occasionally, until the vegetables are turning golden.

2 Add the beer and stock and bring to the boil. Reduce the heat to its lowest setting and add the barley, potato, thyme and mustard. Cover with a lid and cook gently for about 40 minutes, stirring occasionally, until thickened and the barley is just tender. If the stew dries out a bit, add a little water as the dumplings will absorb some of the liquid as they cook. Season to taste with salt and pepper.

3 Make the dumplings. Put the flour, suet and a little salt and pepper in a bowl. Add 150 ml (¼ pint) cold water and stir with a round-bladed knife to make a soft dough.

4 Take dessertspoonfuls of the dough and spoon over the stew. Re-cover and cook for a further 20 minutes until the dumplings are light and fluffy.

Goulash with CHIVE DUMPLINGS

V

4 tablespoons vegetable oil
8 baby onions, peeled
2 garlic cloves, crushed
1 carrot, chopped
1 large celery stick, sliced
500 g (1 lb) potatoes, cubed
1 teaspoon caraway seeds
1 teaspoon smoked paprika
400 g (13 oz) can chopped tomatoes
450 ml (3/4 pint) Vegetable Stock (see page 246)
salt and pepper

Chive dumplings
75 g (3 oz) self-raising flour
1/2 teaspoon salt
50 g (2 oz) vegetable suet
1 tablespoon chopped chives

Serves **4**
Prep time **20 minutes**
Cooking time **50 minutes**

1 Heat the oil in a large saucepan, add the onions, garlic, carrot, celery, potatoes and caraway seeds and cook over a medium heat for 10 minutes, stirring frequently. Add the paprika and cook, stirring, for 1 minute.

2 Stir in the tomatoes, stock and salt and pepper to taste. Bring to the boil, then reduce the heat, cover with a lid and simmer gently for 20 minutes.

3 Make the dumplings. Sift the flour and salt into a bowl and stir in the suet, chives and pepper to taste. Working quickly and lightly, gradually mix in 4–5 tablespoons water to form a soft dough. Divide into eight equal-sized pieces and roll into balls.

4 Carefully arrange the dumplings in the stew, leaving gaps between them, re-cover and simmer for 15 minutes until doubled in size and light and fluffy.

Lentil & Parsnip
COTTAGE PIE

1 tablespoon vegetable oil
1 large onion, chopped
2 celery sticks, finely sliced
4 carrots, chopped
250 g (8 oz) chestnut mushrooms, chopped
2 x 400 g (13 oz) cans green lentils in water, rinsed and drained
400 g (13 oz) can chopped tomatoes
1 tablespoon tomato purée
300 ml (½ pint) Vegetable Stock (see page 246)
2 teaspoons dried mixed herbs
500 g (1 lb) parsnips, peeled and chopped
500 g (1 lb) floury potatoes, peeled and chopped
2 tablespoons milk
25 g (1 oz) butter
50 g (2 oz) mature Cheddar cheese, grated
salt and pepper

Serves 6
Prep time 20 minutes
Cooking time 45 minutes

1 Heat the oil in a large saucepan, add the onion, celery and carrots and cook for 3–4 minutes until softened. Increase the heat, stir in the mushrooms and cook for a further 3 minutes, stirring occasionally.

2 Add the lentils, tomatoes, tomato purée, stock and dried herbs. Bring to the boil, then reduce the heat and simmer, uncovered, for 15 minutes. Season to taste with salt and pepper. Transfer to a 2 litre (3¼ pint) ovenproof dish.

3 Meanwhile, cook the parsnips and potatoes in a large saucepan of lightly salted boiling water for 20 minutes or until tender. Drain the root vegetables and return to the pan. Mash with the milk and butter, then season to taste with salt and pepper.

4 Spoon the parsnip mash over the lentil mixture and scatter over the cheese. Bake in a preheated oven, 190°C (375°F), Gas Mark 5, for 20 minutes until golden and bubbling.

LENTIL BOLOGNESE

1 Finely chop the onion, carrot, celery and garlic. (You can do this in a food processor, if you have one.)

2 Heat the oil in a large, heavy-based casserole or saucepan, add the vegetable mixture and cook for 5-6 minutes, stirring frequently, until softened and lightly golden.

3 Pour in the red wine, 100 ml (3½ fl oz) water, the tomato purée, chopped tomatoes and herbs, then season to taste with salt and pepper. Bring to the boil, then reduce the heat and simmer gently for about 15 minutes.

4 Add the lentils and simmer for a further 5-7 minutes until thickened and tender. Spoon into warmed deep bowls, sprinkle with cheese and serve with plenty of fresh, crusty bread.

1 onion, roughly chopped
1 carrot, roughly chopped
1 celery stick, roughly chopped
1 garlic clove, peeled
3 tablespoons vegetable oil
125 ml (4 fl oz) red wine
75 g (3 oz) tomato purée
400 g (13 oz) can chopped tomatoes
1 teaspoon dried mixed herbs
2 x 400 g (13 oz) cans green lentils, rinsed and drained
salt and pepper

To serve
50 g (2 oz) Parmesan-style cheese, grated
crusty bread

Serves **4**
Prep time **10 minutes**
Cooking time **25-30 minutes**

Creative LEFTOVERS

The word 'leftovers' doesn't exactly conjure up images of culinary delights but when you're eating on a budget you need to make sure you use all the food you buy and come up with clever ways to liven up leftovers. You probably wouldn't think twice about zapping the remains of last night's pizza in the microwave for a mid-morning snack, so there's no excuse for throwing away perfectly good vegetables, fruit or pasta simply because you cooked too much.

KEEP IT COOL

If you're keeping food to use the next day, it's important to let it cool, then cover it and keep it in the fridge so it stays fresh. Don't worry if you only have a small amount of one or two ingredients – you can combine them to make a whole dish, or add them to an existing recipe. It's best to use up leftovers the following day: if you happen to find something lurking in a bowl in the back of the fridge, always check with your housemates how long it's been there – economizing is great but not at the risk of food poisoning.

SLICE IT UP

Leftovers are ideal for soups, stews and curries. With a good selection of spices, vegetable stock cubes and curry pastes in the cupboards and a ready supply of chopped tomatoes, the key is to think of a dish that includes the ingredients you have, rather than just reheating your leftovers and piling them on a plate. There are a few ideas below to give you some inspiration.

QUICK FIXES FOR LEFTOVERS

- Make potato cakes with leftover mash.
- Slice leftover roast potatoes to make a potato bake or dauphinoise.
- Mix cooked, cold pasta with a spoon of pesto or mayonnaise for a quick pasta salad.
- Most vegetables can be puréed to make a soup or chopped for a spicy curry.
- Use leftover rice to make a jambalaya or fried rice dish.
- Use leftover vegetables and pasta to make a pasta bake – top with grated cheese and breadcrumbs.
- Slightly overripe bananas are perfect for banana bread or muffins.
- Any combination of green beans, asparagus, broccoli, potato and peppers can be used to make a frittata.
- If your loaf of bread has seen better days, try a bread and butter pudding – cheap, easy and delicious.
- Chop leftover vegetables and add to steamed couscous.

BUTTERED CAULIFLOWER CRUMBLE

1 large cauliflower
25 g (1 oz) butter
50 g (2 oz) fresh breadcrumbs
2 tablespoons olive oil
3 tablespoons capers, drained
3 cocktail gherkins, finely chopped
3 tablespoons chopped dill or tarragon
100 g (3½ oz) crème fraîche
4 tablespoons grated Parmesan-style cheese
salt and pepper

Serves **4**
Prep time **10 minutes**
Cooking time **15 minutes**

1 Cut the cauliflower into large florets and blanch in a saucepan boiling water for 2 minutes. Drain thoroughly.

2 Melt half of the butter in a large frying pan. Add the breadcrumbs and fry for 2 minutes until golden. Drain and set aside.

3 Melt the remaining butter in the pan with the oil. Add the cauliflower florets and fry gently for about 5 minutes until golden. Add the capers, gherkins, dill or tarragon and crème fraîche, season to taste with salt and pepper and stir over a medium heat for 1 minute.

4 Turn into a shallow flameproof dish and sprinkle with the fried breadcrumbs and grated cheese. Cook under a preheated medium grill for about 2 minutes until the crumbs are dark golden brown.

ROMANESCO
Cauliflower Cheese

8 baby romanescos or 500 g (1 lb) large cauliflower florets
40 g (1½ oz) butter, plus extra for greasing
500 ml (17 fl oz) milk
40 g (1½ oz) plain flour
2 bay leaves
pinch of grated nutmeg
300 g (10 oz) mature farmhouse Cheddar, grated
4 tablespoons grated Parmesan-style cheese
salt and pepper

Serves **4**
Prep time **10 minutes**
Cooking time **20–25 minutes**

1 If using romanescos, trim the base of each to flatten. Lightly grease a shallow flameproof dish.

2 Make the sauce. Melt the butter in a heavy-based saucepan. Gently heat the milk in a separate saucepan. Stir the flour into the melted butter and cook over a low heat for 2–3 minutes, stirring occasionally. Remove the pan from the heat and pour in a little of the warmed milk, stirring constantly. Gradually add the rest of the milk, again stirring constantly. Add the bay leaves and nutmeg and season well. Return the pan to a low heat and cook for 10–12 minutes (or until there is no taste of flour), stirring frequently. Remove the bay leaves. Stir in the Cheddar and remove from the heat.

3 Meanwhile, cook the cauliflower in a saucepan of boiling water for about 5–6 minutes. Drain well, then place in the dish and pour over the sauce.

4 Sprinkle over the Parmesan-style cheese and cook under a preheated medium-high grill for 1 minute until lightly browned. Serve immediately.

GARDENER'S PIE

750 g (1½ lb) small new potatoes
3 tablespoons vegetable oil
1 onion, chopped
1 celery stick, chopped
2 garlic cloves, chopped
3 tablespoons homemade (see page 249) or ready-made pesto
500 g (1 lb) ripe tomatoes, diced
150 ml (¼ pint) hot Vegetable Stock (see page 246) or water
400 g (13 oz) can borlotti or haricot beans, rinsed and drained
125 g (4 oz) fresh or frozen green beans (thawed if frozen), cut into 2.5 cm (1 inch) lengths
50 g (2 oz) Parmesan-style cheese, grated
salt and pepper

Serves **4**
Prep time **15 minutes**
Cooking time **20 minutes**

1 Cook the new potatoes in a saucepan of lightly salted boiling water for about 10 minutes until just tender. Drain and cool slightly, then cut into 5 mm (¼ inch) slices.

2 Meanwhile, heat 2 tablespoons of the oil in a large frying pan, add the onion and cook for 2 minutes. Add the celery and cook for a further 2 minutes, then add the garlic and continue to cook for 2–3 minutes, stirring frequently, until lightly golden.

3 Stir the pesto into the onions, then add the diced tomatoes, stock or water, borlotti or haricot beans and green beans. Season generously with salt and pepper and bring to the boil, then reduce the heat and simmer for 5 minutes until the tomatoes soften and the beans are tender.

4 Tip the vegetable mixture into a large flameproof dish and arrange the sliced potatoes over the top. Sprinkle with the grated cheese, drizzle with the remaining oil and cook under a preheated grill for 7–8 minutes until golden.

GNOCCHI WITH SAGE BUTTER

1 Cook the potatoes in a saucepan of lightly salted boiling water for 10-12 minutes until tender. Drain, return the potatoes to the pan and heat gently for several seconds to dry out.

2 Mash the potatoes and beat in the egg, salt, oil and flour to form a sticky dough. Take walnut-sized pieces of the dough and roll into egg shapes, rolling them over the tines of a fork.

3 Bring a large saucepan of lightly salted water to a rolling boil, add half the gnocchi (freeze the remainder for later use) and cook for 3 minutes until they rise to the surface. Drain the gnocchi and transfer to serving bowls.

4 Meanwhile, melt the butter in a frying pan. As soon as it stops foaming, add the sage and fry over a medium-high heat, stirring, for 2-3 minutes until crisp and the butter turns golden brown. Drizzle over the gnocchi, scatter with grated cheese and serve immediately.

500 g (1 lb) floury potatoes, cubed
1 egg, beaten
1 teaspoon sea salt
2 tablespoons olive oil
175 g (6 oz) plain flour
125 g (4 oz) butter
2 tablespoons chopped sage
salt
grated Parmesan-style cheese, to serve

Serves **4**
Prep time **30 minutes**
Cooking time **20 minutes**

POTATO & ONION PIZZA

3 tablespoons olive oil, plus extra for greasing
300 g (10 oz) plain flour
1 x 7 g (¼ oz) sachet of fast-action dried yeast
1 ½ teaspoons caster sugar
1 teaspoon salt
125 ml (4 fl oz) crème fraîche
200 g (7 oz) unpeeled new potatoes, very thinly sliced
½ onion, very thinly sliced
2 teaspoons dried thyme
100 g (3½ oz) Emmental or Cheddar cheese, grated
12 pitted black olives (optional)
pepper

Serves 4
Prep time **20 minutes**
Cooking time **20 minutes**

1 Lightly oil a baking sheet. In a large bowl, mix together the flour, yeast, sugar and salt. Make a well in the centre and pour in 175 ml (6 fl oz) warm water and 2 tablespoons of the oil. Combine to make a soft dough, then roll out to a rectangle about 35 x 25 cm (14 x 10 inches). Transfer to the baking sheet and bake in a preheated oven, 200°C (400°F), Gas Mark 6, for 5 minutes or until just beginning to colour.

2 Spoon 4 tablespoons of the crème fraîche over the pizza base. Top with the slices of potato and onion, then sprinkle over the thyme and scatter with the cheese. Drizzle the remaining oil over the pizza and return to the oven. Increase the temperature to 220°C (425°F), Gas Mark 7, and bake for about 15 minutes until golden.

3 Cut the pizza into slices, scatter with the olives, if using, and top with the remaining crème fraîche. Season with pepper and serve hot.

Roasted & Baked

BEAN & POTATO MOUSSAKA

CHEESE, TOMATO & BASIL MUFFINS

60 STUFFED RED ONIONS

61 FETA-STUFFED PEPPERS

62 GRILLED PEPPERS WITH GOATS' CHEESE

63 BROCCOLI & SPINACH EGGAHS

64 BROCCOLI & BLUE CHEESE SOUFFLÉS

65 BUTTERNUT & AUBERGINE TIKKA

66 BEAN & POTATO MOUSSAKA

68 MELANZANE PARMIGIANA

69 CHUNKY PEANUT ROAST WITH HOMEMADE COLESLAW

70 RED ONION, ROSEMARY & GRUYÈRE TOAD

71 TRICOLORE CAULIFLOWER GRATIN

72 SPINACH & POTATO GRATIN
73 BUTTER BEAN & VEGETABLE NUT CRUMBLE
76 ROOT VEGETABLE & BEAN CRUMBLE
77 CHEESY LENTIL & VEGETABLE PIE
78 MOROCCAN-STYLE SWEET POTATO PIE
79 FILO, PESTO & MOZZARELLA PARCELS
80 TOFU, CINNAMON & HONEY PARCELS
81 LEEK & MUSHROOM PASTIES
82 RED ONION & GOATS' CHEESE TART
84 MARGHERITA TART
85 CHERRY TOMATO TARTS WITH PESTO CRÈME FRAÎCHE
86 CHEESE, TOMATO & BASIL MUFFINS
87 CHEESE & HERB SCONES
88 CHEAT'S MEDITERRANEAN FOCACCIA
90 SPICED FLATBREADS
91 MIXED SEED SODA BREAD
92 BLACKBERRY MUFFIN SLICE
94 LEMON DRIZZLE CAKE
95 VICTORIA SANDWICH CAKE
96 VEGAN BANANA PECAN CAKE WITH CARAMEL TOPPING
97 CHOCOLATE FUDGE CAKE
98 LEMON POPPING CANDY CAKES
99 VEGAN CHILLI & LIME CHOCOLATE MUFFINS
100 CHOCOLATE MOCHA BROWNIES
102 CHOCOLATE CHIP COOKIES
103 CHEWY OAT & RAISIN BARS
104 CRUMBLY RASPBERRY & OAT SLICES
105 CRANBERRY, OATMEAL & CINNAMON SCONES

CHEAT'S MEDITERRANEAN FOCACCIA

Stuffed RED ONIONS

4 large red onions, peeled
2 tablespoons olive oil
125 g (4 oz) button mushrooms, finely chopped
75 g (3 oz) bulgar wheat
1 tablespoon chopped parsley
1 tablespoon sultanas
1 tablespoon grated Parmesan-style cheese (optional)
salt and pepper

Serves 4
Prep time 30 minutes
Cooking time 1 ½ hours

1 Cut the top off each onion and scoop out the centres using a teaspoon. Heat the oil in a frying pan. Finely chop the scooped-out onion, then add to the pan and fry until soft and golden brown. Add the mushrooms and cook, stirring, for a further 5 minutes.

2 Meanwhile, bring a large pan of water to the boil. Add the onion cups and simmer for 10 minutes or until they begin to soften. Drain well.

3 Add the bulgar, parsley, salt, pepper and 300 ml (½ pint) water to the mushrooms. Boil for 5 minutes. Cover the pan and simmer for a further 30 minutes or until the grains have softened. Add extra water if needed.

4 Stir the sultanas into the bulgar mixture and spoon into the onions. Put the onions in a roasting tin and cover with foil. Cook in a preheated oven, 190°C (375°F), Gas Mark 5, for 30 minutes. Remove the foil, sprinkle over the cheese, if using, and cook for a further 10 minutes.

FETA-STUFFED PEPPERS

150 g (5 oz) bulgar wheat
800 ml (1 pint 7 fl oz) Vegetable Stock (see page 246)
2 orange peppers
2 yellow peppers
40 g (1½ oz) sultanas
¼ teaspoon ground allspice
100 g (3½ oz) feta cheese, crumbled
1 small bunch of basil, torn
3 tablespoons olive oil
1 onion, chopped
3 garlic cloves, finely chopped
500 g (1 lb) tomatoes, roughly chopped
salt and pepper

Serves 4
Prep time **20 minutes**
Cooking time **45 minutes**

1 Cook the bulgar wheat in 600 ml (1 pint) of the stock in a covered saucepan for 10 minutes.

2 Lay each pepper on a chopping board and make a cut from the base up towards and around the stem, opening out enough to remove the core and seeds but not so much that the pepper splits in two.

3 Drain off any excess stock from the cooked bulgar, add the sultanas, allspice, feta, a little of the basil and some salt and pepper. Mix together and spoon into the peppers. Transfer to a roasting tin.

4 Heat 1 tablespoon of the oil in a frying pan, add the onion and fry for 5 minutes until lightly browned. Add the garlic, tomatoes, remaining stock and a little salt and pepper. Spoon around the peppers and sprinkle with a little more torn basil.

5 Drizzle the peppers with the remaining oil and cook in a preheated oven, 200°C (400°F), Gas Mark 6, for 30 minutes or until the peppers are softened. Serve garnished with the remaining basil.

Baked Peppers
WITH GOATS' CHEESE

4 red peppers, halved, cored and deseeded
400 g (13 oz) can flageolet beans, rinsed and drained
4 teaspoons olive oil
125 g (4 oz) firm goats' cheese
8 teaspoons homemade (see page 249) or ready-made pesto

Serves **4**
Prep time **5 minutes**
Cooking time **30 minutes**

1 Put the pepper halves on a baking sheet, skin side down, and divide the flageolet beans among them. Drizzle with the oil.

2 Cut the goats' cheese horizontally into 2 slices and arrange them on top of the peppers. Top each one with 1 teaspoon pesto.

3 Cover the peppers with foil and bake in a preheated oven, 200°C (400°F), Gas Mark 6, for 20 minutes or until the peppers are tender. Remove the foil and bake for a further 10 minutes.

BROCCOLI & SPINACH EGGAHS

vegetable oil, for greasing
125 g (4 oz) broccoli
100 g (3½ oz) baby spinach leaves
6 eggs
300 ml (½ pint) semi-skimmed milk
2 tablespoons grated Parmesan-style cheese
large pinch of ground nutmeg
salt and pepper

Makes **12**
Prep time **15 minutes**
Cooking time **20 minutes**

1 Lightly oil the holes of a deep 12-hole muffin tin. Cut the broccoli into small florets and thickly slice the stems. Put in a steamer set over boiling water, cover with a lid and cook for 3 minutes. Add the spinach and cook for 1 minute more or until the spinach has just wilted.

2 Beat the eggs, milk, cheese, nutmeg and a little salt and pepper together in a jug.

3 Divide the broccoli and spinach among the holes of the muffin tin and cover with the egg mixture. Bake in a preheated oven, 190°C (375°F), Gas Mark 5, for about 15 minutes or until lightly browned, well risen and the egg mixture has set. Leave in the tin for 1–2 minutes, then loosen the edges with a knife and turn out.

BROCCOLI & BLUE CHEESE SOUFFLÉS

1 Brush four 300 ml (½ pint) ramekins with melted butter and sprinkle with breadcrumbs to coat the base and sides.

2 Blanch the broccoli in a saucepan of boiling water until almost tender, then whizz with a stick blender, or a food processor or blender if you have one, until smooth.

3 Melt the butter in a pan, add the flour and cook for 2 minutes. Gradually add the milk, stirring constantly, and bring to the boil. Boil for 2 minutes until very thick. Remove from the heat and stir in the spices and egg yolks. Season well and stir in the puréed broccoli and cheese.

4 In a clean bowl, whisk the egg whites until stiff. Using a metal spoon, carefully fold the egg whites into the broccoli and cheese mixture.

5 Pour into the ramekins, almost up to the rim. Run your finger around the inside edge of the ramekins to help the soufflés rise straight up. Bake on a preheated hot baking sheet in a preheated oven, 200°C (400°F), Gas Mark 6, for 8–10 minutes or until risen. Serve immediately.

50 g (2 oz) butter, plus extra melted butter for greasing
handful of fine fresh white breadcrumbs
250 g (8 oz) broccoli florets
40 g (1 ½ oz) plain flour
300 ml (½ pint) milk
1 teaspoon smoked paprika
pinch of grated nutmeg
4 large eggs, separated
100 g (3 ½ oz) creamy blue cheese, crumbled
salt and pepper

Serves **4**
Prep time **20 minutes**
Cooking time **15 minutes**

AFFORDABILITY 1

Butternut & Aubergine Tikka

- 1 small butternut squash, about 500 g (1 lb), peeled, deseeded and cut into 2.5 cm (1 inch) cubes
- 1 small aubergine, cut into 2.5 cm (1 inch) cubes
- 6 shallots, quartered
- 3 tablespoons vegetable oil
- 2 garlic cloves, finely chopped
- 4 tablespoons tikka masala curry paste (suitable for vegetarians)
- 200 g (7 oz) canned chopped tomatoes
- 1 tablespoon mango chutney
- salt
- 3 tablespoons natural yogurt
- chopped fresh coriander, to garnish
- warmed naan bread or boiled basmati rice, to serve

Serves **2**
Prep time **20 minutes**
Cooking time **1 hour 5 minutes**

1 Scatter the squash in a roasting tin or shallow baking dish with the aubergine and shallots. Drizzle with the oil and bake in a preheated oven, 200°C (400°F), Gas Mark 6, for about 50 minutes, turning the ingredients once or twice, until golden and almost tender.

2 Mix the garlic with the curry paste, tomatoes, chutney and a little salt and spoon into the dish, stirring the vegetables to coat in the sauce.

3 Return to the oven and cook for a further 10 minutes. Stir in the yogurt and continue to cook for 5 minutes until hot and bubbling.

4 Sprinkle with coriander and serve with naan bread or rice.

Bean & Potato MOUSSAKA

750 g (1 ½ lb) equal-sized potatoes, washed
1 tablespoon vegetable oil
1 large onion, chopped
1 garlic clove, crushed
1 large carrot, sliced
1 teaspoon ground cinnamon
2 teaspoons dried mixed herbs
400 g (13 oz) can chopped tomatoes
400 g (13 oz) can red kidney beans, rinsed and drained
300 ml (½ pint) Vegetable Stock (see page 246)
50 g (2 oz) butter
50 g (2 oz) plain flour
600 ml (1 pint) milk
75 g (3 oz) mature Cheddar cheese, grated
1 egg
salt and pepper

Serves **4**
Prep time **15 minutes, plus cooling**
Cooking time **55–60 minutes**

1 Cook the potatoes in a large saucepan of boiling water for about 10 minutes until just tender. Drain and leave until cool enough to handle, then remove the skins and slice into 5 mm (¼ inch) slices.

2 Heat the oil in a large saucepan, add the onion and garlic and cook gently for 3–4 minutes until softened. Add the carrot, cinnamon and herbs, then stir in the tomatoes, kidney beans and stock. Season to taste with salt and pepper and bring to the boil, then reduce the heat and simmer, uncovered, for 15 minutes until thickened.

3 Meanwhile, make the sauce. Place the butter, flour and milk in a saucepan and whisk constantly over a medium heat until the sauce boils and thickens. Simmer for 2-3 minutes until you have a smooth glossy sauce. Stir in the cheese and then remove from the heat. Leave to cool slightly, then beat in the egg.

4 Place half the bean mixture in the bottom of a deep ovenproof dish and top with a layer of potatoes. Repeat, finishing with a layer of potatoes. Pour over the sauce and bake in a preheated oven, 180°C (350°F), Gas Mark 4, for 25–30 minutes until golden brown. Leave to stand for 5 minutes before serving.

Melanzane PARMIGIANA

- 6 aubergines
- 2 tablespoons olive oil
- 2 x 400 g (13 oz) cans chopped tomatoes
- 2 garlic cloves, crushed
- 250 g (8 oz) Cheddar cheese, grated
- 50 g (2 oz) Parmesan-style cheese, grated
- salt and pepper

Serves **6**
Prep time **15 minutes**
Cooking time **50 minutes**

1 Trim the aubergines and cut lengthways into thick slices. Brush them with half the oil and place on two large baking sheets. Roast at the top of a preheated oven, 200°C (400°F), Gas Mark 6, for 10 minutes on each side until golden and tender.

2 Meanwhile, place the tomatoes and garlic in a saucepan and bring to the boil. Reduce the heat and simmer for 10 minutes, then season with salt and pepper.

3 Spoon a little of the tomato into an ovenproof dish and top with a layer of aubergines and some of the Cheddar. Continue with the layers, finishing with a layer of Cheddar on top. Sprinkle over the Parmesan-style cheese and bake for 30 minutes until the cheese is bubbling and golden.

CHUNKY PEANUT ROAST

with homemade coleslaw

1 Heat the oil in a saucepan, add the onions and fry for 5 minutes until softened. Tip into a bowl and add the spices, peanuts, breadcrumbs and coriander. Mix well. Add the eggs to the bowl and stir well until combined.

2 Brush a large square of kitchen foil with oil. Tip the peanut mixture out on to the foil and shape into a log about 18 cm (7 inches) long. Roll the foil up around the log and twist the ends to resemble a wrapped sweet. Bake in a preheated oven, 180°C (350°F), Gas Mark 4, for 25 minutes.

3 Meanwhile, put the cabbage, shallot and parsley in a bowl. Quarter, core and thinly slice the apples and add to the bowl. Mix together the mayonnaise, yogurt and celery seeds or salt, if using, with a little pepper and add to the bowl. Mix well.

4 Serve the peanut roast thickly sliced with the coleslaw.

2 tablespoons vegetable oil, plus extra for greasing
2 red onions, chopped
2 teaspoons paprika
1 teaspoon ground cumin
150 g (5 oz) salted peanuts
100 g (3½ oz) roasted, unsalted peanuts
50 g (2 oz) fresh brown or white breadcrumbs
25 g (1 oz) fresh coriander, chopped
2 eggs, beaten
pepper

Coleslaw
½ small white cabbage, shredded
1 shallot, chopped
3 tablespoons chopped parsley
2 red dessert apples
75 g (3 oz) mayonnaise
75 g (3 oz) natural yogurt
¼ teaspoon celery seeds or celery salt (optional)

Serves **4**
Prep time **25 minutes**
Cooking time **30 minutes**

RED ONION, Rosemary & GRUYÈRE TOAD

625 g (1¼ lb) red onions, quartered
1 tablespoon roughly chopped rosemary
4 tablespoons vegetable oil
125 g (4 oz) plain flour
2 eggs
300 ml (½ pint) milk
150 g (5 oz) Gruyère or Emmental cheese, grated
salt and pepper
green vegetable or baked beans, to serve

Serves 4
Prep time 20 minutes
Cooking time 1 hour

1 Scatter the onions and rosemary in a shallow roasting tin and drizzle with 2 tablespoons of the oil. Mix well and cook in a preheated oven, 200°C (400°F), Gas Mark 6, for 30 minutes until the onions are soft and lightly browned.

2 Meanwhile, put the flour in a bowl and make a well in the centre. Break the eggs into the well with a little of the milk. Whisk the eggs and milk together, gradually working in the flour to make a thick paste. Once the paste is smooth, gradually beat in the remaining milk, a little salt, plenty of pepper and a third of the cheese.

3 Pour the remaining oil around the onions and return to the oven for 5 minutes to get the oil really hot. Pour the batter around the onions and scatter with the remaining cheese. Return to the oven for 25–30 minutes until well risen and golden. Serve with green vegetables or baked beans.

TRICOLORE CAULIFLOWER GRATIN

3 tomatoes, sliced
200 g (7 oz) spinach leaves, tough stalks removed
pinch of grated nutmeg
1 cauliflower, cut into florets
40 g (1½ oz) butter
40 g (1½ oz) plain flour
450 ml (¾ pint) semi-skimmed milk
175 g (6 oz) mature Cheddar cheese, grated
½ slice of bread, torn into tiny pieces
2 tablespoons sunflower seeds
2 tablespoons pumpkin seeds
salt and pepper

Serves 4
Prep time **15 minutes**
Cooking time **30 minutes**

1 Arrange the tomatoes in the base of a shallow ovenproof dish. Steam the spinach for 1–2 minutes until just wilted, then spoon over the tomatoes. Sprinkle with a little nutmeg and some salt and pepper. Steam the cauliflower for 8–10 minutes until just tender.

2 Meanwhile, melt the butter in a separate saucepan and stir in the flour. Gradually whisk in the milk and bring to the boil, stirring constantly, until smooth and thick. Stir in two-thirds of the cheese and season well.

3 Arrange the cauliflower on top of the spinach, then gently mix together. Pour the sauce over the top. Mix the remaining cheese with the torn bread and seeds, then sprinkle over the cheese sauce.

4 Bake in a preheated oven, 200°C (400°F), Gas Mark 6, for 20 minutes until the topping is crisp and golden and the vegetables are piping hot.

SPINACH & POTATO GRATIN

butter, for greasing
625 g (1¼ lb) potatoes, peeled and thinly sliced
500 g (1 lb) spinach leaves, tough stalks removed
200 g (7 oz) mozzarella cheese, grated
4 tomatoes, sliced
3 eggs, beaten
300 ml (½ pint) whipping cream
salt and pepper

Serves 4
Prep time 15 minutes
Cooking time 35 minutes

1 Grease a large ovenproof dish. Cook the potatoes in a large saucepan of salted boiling water for 5 minutes, then drain well.

2 Meanwhile, cook the spinach in a separate saucepan of boiling water for 1–2 minutes. Drain and squeeze out the excess water.

3 Line the bottom of the prepared dish with half the potato slices. Cover with the spinach and half the mozzarella, seasoning each layer well with salt and pepper. Cover with the remaining potato slices and arrange the tomato slices on top. Scatter with the remaining mozzarella.

4 Beat the eggs and cream together in a bowl and season well with salt and pepper. Pour over the ingredients in the dish. Bake in a preheated oven, 180°C (350°F), Gas Mark 4, for about 30 minutes. Serve immediately.

BUTTER BEAN & VEGETABLE NUT CRUMBLE

175 g (6 oz) plain flour
75 g (3 oz) cold butter, diced
100 g (3½ oz) walnuts, chopped
50 g (2 oz) Cheddar cheese, grated
2 x 250 g (8 oz) packs ready-prepared broccoli, cauliflower and carrots
500 g (1 lb) jar ready-made tomato and herb sauce
2 garlic cloves, crushed
6 tablespoons finely chopped basil leaves
400 g (13 oz) can butter beans, rinsed and drained
salt and pepper

Serves **4**
Prep time **15 minutes**
Cooking time **20–25 minutes**

1 Place the flour in a bowl, add the butter and rub in with the fingertips until the mixture resembles breadcrumbs. Stir in the chopped walnuts and grated cheese, season and set aside.

2 Remove the carrots from the packs of prepared vegetables, roughly chop and boil for 2 minutes. Add the broccoli and cauliflower and cook for another minute, then drain.

3 Meanwhile, heat the tomato and herb sauce in a large saucepan until bubbling. Stir in the garlic, basil, butter beans and blanched vegetables.

4 Transfer the bean mixture to a medium-sized ovenproof dish and scatter over the crumble. Bake in a preheated oven, 200°C (400°F), Gas Mark 6, for 15–20 minutes or until golden and bubbling.

AFFORDABILITY 2

STUDENT TIP

Look out for discount vouchers in local papers and take advantage of online shopping deals from the big retailers. Many have introductory offers for new customers – but that doesn't mean you have to continue shopping with them once you've taken advantage of the deals.

Dinner Dates WITH MATES

Although much of your socializing will involve alcoholic drinks washed down with the odd packet of crisps or nuts, you might occasionally want to leave the gloomy interior of your local pub and host a gathering at home. The days of formal dinner parties are long gone, which ties in nicely with the less salubrious nature of student life, and you don't need to be a gourmet chef to put together a decent meal. Nobody will expect Michelin Stars to light up the dining table; in fact, many of your friends will be so grateful for a free meal that any culinary catastrophes will be totally overlooked.

MISMATCH CHIC

These days, trendy hosts are leaving their posh dinner plates gathering dust in the attic and are instead laying the table with an eclectic mix of crockery, cutlery and decorations. As a student, you probably won't have much choice in the matter and, depending on numbers, you might have to borrow extra knives, forks and plates for your dinner party. A few flowers in jam jars or mismatched candles will complete the shabby-chic look and you can hold your head up high as a trendsetter.

LOVE THE LIST

If shopping tends to involve ad hoc visits to the convenience store, you'll need to be more organized if you're inviting people round for dinner. Start by choosing your menu. Forget the traditional three-course affair with coffee and a cheese course; you're looking for low-maintenance meals that you can ideally prep in advance. That way, you can do all the sweating, swearing and kitchen full of smoke well before your mates arrive and be the perfect stress-free hostess at dinnertime. If you want to make a starter, choose something that can be plated up ahead of time and served cold. Likewise pick a pud that's easy to dish up after a few glasses of wine – or buy a selection of ice creams.

Write a list of all the ingredients you need and go to a large supermarket to make sure you can get everything in one shopping trip. If you're shopping a day or two ahead of your gathering, make sure you check the use-by dates so you don't end up with a key ingredient going to waste. If you share cupboard or fridge space with your housemates, let them know that your recent purchases are strictly out of bounds for drunken raids.

CONVERTING THE CARNIVORES

Don't forget that you might be inviting hardened carnivores to your dining table: treat them gently by keeping your menu simple and recognizable. It might be doing them a disservice to say they'll turn their noses up at quinoa or sprouting beans, but meat lovers can be a little less adventurous when it comes to veggie food. The idea is to showcase meat-free meals, not put people off.

ROOT VEGETABLE & BEAN CRUMBLE

1 Heat the oil in a large saucepan, add the carrots, parsnips and leeks and cook over a medium heat for 4–5 minutes until slightly softened.

2 Stir the wine into the pan and cook until reduced by half, then stir in the tomatoes, stock, butter beans and rosemary. Season well with salt and pepper, then cover with a lid and simmer for 15 minutes, stirring occasionally. Transfer to a 2 litre (3½ pint) ovenproof dish.

3 Meanwhile, make the crumble topping. Place the bread, walnuts, parsley and 75 g (3 oz) of the cheese in a food processor and pulse until the mixture resembles breadcrumbs. Alternatively, whizz the ingredients in batches using a stick blender.

4 Spoon the topping over the vegetable mixture and scatter over the remaining cheese. Bake in a preheated oven, 180°C (350°F), Gas Mark 4, for 25–30 minutes until golden and crisp.

1 tablespoon olive oil
2 carrots, sliced
2 parsnips, peeled and chopped
2 leeks, trimmed and sliced
300 ml (½ pint) red wine
400 g (13 oz) can chopped tomatoes
300 ml (½ pint) Vegetable Stock (see page 246)
400 g (13 oz) can butter beans, rinsed and drained
1 tablespoon chopped rosemary
salt and pepper

Crumble topping
100 g (3½ oz) sliced wholemeal bread, roughly torn into pieces
50 g (2 oz) walnuts, roughly chopped
2 tablespoons chopped flat leaf parsley
100 g (3½ oz) Wensleydale or Lancashire cheese, crumbled

Serves **4–6**
Prep time **20 minutes**
Cooking time **50–55 minutes**

CHEESY LENTIL & VEGETABLE PIE

THE POTATOES AND CABBAGE IN THIS RECIPE ARE COOKED IN A STEAMER, WHICH RETAINS MORE NUTRIENTS THAN BOILING. IF YOU DON'T HAVE A STEAMER, BOIL THE VEGETABLES IN AS LITTLE WATER AS POSSIBLE AND ONLY ADD THEM WHEN THE WATER IS PIPING HOT.

1 tablespoon vegetable oil
1 onion, finely chopped
500 g (1 lb) carrots, diced
2 garlic cloves, finely chopped
415 g (14 oz) can low-sugar, low-salt baked beans
125 g (4 oz) red lentils
450 ml (3/4 pint) Vegetable Stock (see page 246)
salt and pepper

Topping
750 g (1½ lb) baking potatoes
150 g (5 oz) Savoy cabbage, finely shredded
3–4 tablespoons semi-skimmed milk
100 g (3 ½ oz) Cheddar cheese, grated

Serves **4**
Prep time **30 minutes**
Cooking time **35 minutes**

1 Heat the oil in a saucepan, add the onion and cook for about 5 minutes, stirring occasionally, until softened. Stir in the carrots and garlic and cook for 2 minutes.

2 Mix in the baked beans, lentils and stock and season to taste. Bring to the boil, then reduce the heat, cover with a lid and simmer for 20 minutes until the lentils are tender, adding extra liquid if necessary.

3 Meanwhile, make the topping. Cut the potatoes into large chunks and cook them in the base of a steamer, half-filled with boiling water, for 15 minutes. Add the steamer top, fill with the cabbage, cover with a lid and cook for 5 minutes until both cabbage and potatoes are tender.

4 Drain the potatoes, return them to the pan and mash with the milk. Stir in the cabbage and two-thirds of the cheese.

5 Spoon the hot carrot mixture into the base of a 1.5 litre (2½ pint) flameproof pie dish. Spoon the potato mixture on top, then sprinkle with the remaining cheese. Place under a preheated hot grill for 5 minutes until golden brown.

MOROCCAN-STYLE SWEET POTATO *Pie*

2 tablespoons vegetable oil
1 large onion, roughly chopped
1 large fennel bulb, roughly chopped
1 tablespoon ras el hanout Moroccan spice blend
2 garlic cloves, chopped
2 teaspoons plain flour
800 g (1 lb 10 oz) sweet potatoes, scrubbed and cut into 1.5 cm (3/4 inch) chunks
500 ml (17 fl oz) Vegetable Stock (see page 246)
50 g (2 oz) dried pitted dates, roughly chopped
3 tablespoons chopped mint
500 g (1 lb) puff pastry (thawed if frozen)
flour, for dusting
beaten egg, or milk, to glaze
salt and pepper

Serves **4**
Prep time **25 minutes, plus cooling**
Cooking time **1 hour**

1 Heat the oil in a saucepan or large frying pan, add the onion and fennel and gently fry for 5 minutes until softened. Stir in the spice blend, garlic and flour and cook for another 1 minute.

2 Add the sweet potatoes and stock and bring to the boil. Reduce the heat to its lowest setting, cover with a lid and cook gently for 15 minutes. Stir in the dates and mint, season to taste with salt and pepper and leave to cool.

3 Turn the mixture into a pie dish. Roll out the pastry on a lightly floured surface until large enough to cover the pie dish. Brush the edges of the dish with water and lift the lid into position, pressing the pastry firmly around the rim. Trim off the excess pastry and make a hole in the centre of the pie for the steam to escape.

4 Brush the top of the pastry with beaten egg or milk and bake in a preheated oven, 200°C (400°F), Gas Mark 6, for 35 minutes until the pastry is risen and deep golden.

FILO, PESTO &
MOZZARELLA PARCELS

UNFORTUNATELY, FILO PASTRY SHEETS VARY CONSIDERABLY IN SIZE, SO BEAR THIS IN MIND WHEN SHAPING IT INTO PARCELS. AS LONG AS THE CHEESE IS WRAPPED IN A DOUBLE THICKNESS OF OVERLAPPING FILO, IT SHOULD NOT SEEP OUT DURING BAKING.

125 g (4 oz) filo pastry sheets
about 50 g (2 oz) butter, melted
3 tablespoons homemade (see page 249) or ready-made red pesto
250 g (8 oz) mozzarella cheese, sliced
50 g (2 oz) Parmesan-style cheese, grated
salt and pepper
leafy salad, to serve

Serves 4
Prep time **15 minutes**
Cooking time **10 minutes**

1 Cut the filo pastry into 16 x 15 cm (6 inch) squares. Lay eight squares on a clean work surface and brush with a little melted butter. Cover each with a second square.

2 Dot the pesto into the centres of the squares and spread slightly. Arrange the cheese over the pesto. Season lightly with salt and pepper.

3 Bring two opposite sides of the pastry over the filling to enclose completely. Lightly brush with butter, then fold over the two open ends to make parcels. Place on a baking sheet with the ends uppermost. Repeat with the remaining pastries.

4 Brush with the remaining butter (melt a little more if necessary) and bake in a preheated oven, 200°C (400°F), Gas Mark 6, for about 10 minutes until golden. Serve warm with a leafy salad.

Tofu, Cinnamon & HONEY PARCELS

1 Melt half of the butter in a frying pan, add the onions and fry for 3 minutes until softened. Stir in the almonds and fry for 2 minutes until turning golden. Stir in the honey, cinnamon and tofu, then season to taste with salt and pepper.

2 Melt the remaining butter in a small saucepan. Cut out 16 x 18 cm (7 inch) squares from the filo pastry. Lay eight squares on a clean work surface and brush with a little melted butter. Cover each with a second square placed at an angle to create a star shape. Pile the tofu mixture on to the centres of the squares.

3 Brush the edges of the pastry with a little butter. Bring the edges up over the filling and pinch together to make bundles. Repeat with the remaining pastries. Transfer to a baking sheet and brush with the remaining butter.

4 Bake in a preheated oven, 200°C (400°F), Gas Mark 6, for about 10 minutes until the pastry is golden. Serve warm.

50 g (2 oz) butter
2 onions, chopped
50 g (2 oz) flaked almonds, lightly crushed
1 tablespoon clear honey
1 teaspoon ground cinnamon
200 g (7 oz) tofu, diced
150 g (5 oz) filo pastry sheets
salt and pepper

Serves **4**
Prep time **15 minutes**
Cooking time **15 minutes**

LEEK & MUSHROOM PASTIES

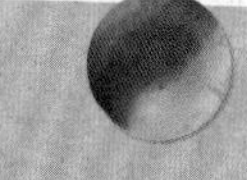

50 g (2 oz) butter
2 leeks, trimmed and sliced
500 g (1 lb) mushrooms, halved (or quartered, if very large)
200 g (7 oz) cream cheese
1 teaspoon dried tarragon or 1 tablespoon chopped fresh tarragon
500 g (1 lb) puff pastry (thawed if frozen)
flour, for dusting
beaten egg, to glaze
salt and pepper

Serves 4
Prep time **15 minutes**
Cooking time **25–30 minutes**

1 Melt the butter in a large frying pan, add the leeks and cook over a medium heat for 3 minutes, stirring occasionally, until they begin to soften. Add the mushrooms and continue to cook for a further 4–5 minutes until tender and lightly golden, then stir in the cream cheese and tarragon.

2 Meanwhile, roll out the pastry on a lightly floured surface and cut into four 20 cm (8 inch) circles. Brush a 1 cm (½ inch) border with a little beaten egg.

3 Season the leek and mushrooms with a pinch each of salt and pepper and divide the mixture between the circles. Now bring up two sides of the pastry to encase the filling, crimping the pastry together with your fingers to seal the edges. Repeat to make four pasties.

4 Place the pasties on a baking sheet, brush with the remaining beaten egg and cook in a preheated oven, 200°C (400°F), Gas Mark 6, for about 18 minutes until puffed up and golden. Serve warm.

Red Onion and GOATS' CHEESE tart

25 g (1 oz) butter
4 large red onions, thinly sliced
1 teaspoon soft light brown sugar
2 tablespoons chopped thyme, plus a few extra leaves to garnish
2 teaspoons balsamic vinegar
320 g (10½ oz) sheet of ready-rolled puff pastry (thawed if frozen)
2 x 100 g (3½ oz) round goats' cheeses, each sliced into 4

Serves **4**
Prep time **10 minutes, plus cooling**
Cooking time **40 minutes**

1 Melt the butter in a large frying pan, add the onions, sugar and chopped thyme and cook gently for 20 minutes, stirring occasionally, until the onions start to caramelize. Stir in the vinegar and cook for 1 minute. Leave to cool slightly.

2 Unroll the pastry sheet and place on a nonstick baking sheet. Using a sharp knife, score a line along each side of the sheet 2.5 cm (1 inch) from the edge, being careful not to cut all the way through the pastry.

3 Spoon the caramelized onions over the pastry, within the scored border, then top with the goats' cheese slices. Bake in a preheated oven, 200°C (400°F), Gas Mark 6, for 20 minutes until the pastry is risen and golden. Serve garnished with a few thyme leaves.

MARGHERITA TART

1 Unroll the sheet of pastry on a lined or lightly greased baking sheet and lightly score a 1.5 cm (3/4 inch) border around the edge.

2 Spread the pesto evenly over the base, working within the border. Arrange the cherry tomatoes and mozzarella over the pesto, then scatter over the olives and oregano, if using.

3 Drizzle with the oil and bake in a preheated oven, 190°C (375°F), Gas Mark 5, for 20–25 minutes until the pastry is crisp and golden. Cut into squares and serve with a rocket salad, if liked.

375 g (12 oz) sheet of ready-rolled puff pastry (thawed if frozen)
2 teaspoons olive oil, plus extra for greasing
3 tablespoons homemade (see page 249) or ready-made green or red pesto
300 g (10 oz) cherry tomatoes, halved (or regular tomatoes, sliced)
125 g (4 oz) mozzarella cheese, torn or sliced
12 pitted green or black olives in brine, rinsed and drained (optional)
1 teaspoon dried oregano (optional)
rocket salad, to serve (optional)

Serves **4**
Prep time **5 minutes**
Cooking time **20–25 minutes**

CHERRY TOMATO
TARTS WITH PESTO CRÈME FRAÎCHE

2 tablespoons olive oil, plus extra for greasing
1 onion, finely chopped
375 g (12 oz) cherry tomatoes
2 garlic cloves, crushed
3 tablespoons sun-dried tomato paste
325 g (11 oz) puff pastry (thawed if frozen)
flour, for dusting
beaten egg, to glaze
150 g (5 oz) crème fraîche
2 tablespoons homemade (see page 249) or ready-made pesto
salt and pepper
basil leaves, to garnish

Serves **4**
Prep time **10 minutes**
Cooking time **20 minutes**

1 Lightly oil a large baking sheet and sprinkle with water. Heat the oil in a frying pan, add the onion and fry for about 3 minutes until softened. Halve about 150 g (5 oz) of the tomatoes. Remove the pan from the heat, add the garlic and sun-dried tomato paste, then stir in all the tomatoes, turning until they are lightly coated in the sauce.

2 Roll out the pastry on a lightly floured surface and cut out four 12 cm (5 inch) rounds, using a cutter or small bowl as a guide. Transfer to the baking sheet and make a shallow cut 1 cm (½ inch) from the edge of each round using the tip of a sharp knife to form a rim. (Do not cut all the way through the pastry.) Brush the rims with beaten egg. Pile the tomato mixture on to the centres of the pastries, making sure the mixture stays within the rims. Bake in a preheated oven, 220°C (425°F), Gas Mark 7, for about 15 minutes until the pastry is risen and golden.

3 Meanwhile, lightly mix together the crème fraîche, pesto and salt and pepper in a bowl so that the crème fraîche is streaked with the pesto.

4 Transfer the cooked tarts to warmed plates and spoon over the crème fraîche pesto. Serve scattered with basil leaves.

Cheese, Tomato & Basil Muffins

1 Lightly oil eight holes of a muffin tin. Sift the flour and salt into a bowl and stir in the cornmeal, 50 g (2 oz) of the cheese, the tomatoes and basil. Make a well in the centre.

2 Beat the egg, milk and oil together in a separate bowl or jug, pour into the well and stir together until just combined. The batter should remain a little lumpy.

3 Divide the batter among the holes of the muffin tin and scatter over the remaining cheese. Bake in a preheated oven, 180°C (350°F), Gas Mark 4, for 20–25 minutes until risen and golden. Leave to cool in the tin for 5 minutes, then transfer to a wire rack to cool. Serve warm with butter.

2 tablespoons olive oil, plus extra for greasing
150 g (5 oz) self-raising flour
½ teaspoon salt
100 g (3 ½ oz) fine cornmeal
65 g (2 ½ oz) Cheddar cheese, grated
50 g (2 oz) drained sun-dried tomatoes in oil, chopped
2 tablespoons chopped basil
1 egg, lightly beaten
300 ml (½ pint) milk
butter, to serve

Makes **8**
Prep time **10 minutes**
Cooking time **20-25 minutes**

CHEESE & HERB SCONES

250 g (8 oz) self-raising flour, plus extra for dusting
75 g (3 oz) unsalted butter, diced
4 tablespoons grated Parmesan-style cheese
3 tablespoons chopped mixed fresh herbs, such as oregano and chives
1 egg, lightly beaten
2 tablespoons buttermilk

Makes **12**
Prep time **10 minutes**
Cooking time **10-12 minutes**

1 Sift the flour into a large bowl, add the butter and rub in with the fingertips until the mixture resembles fine breadcrumbs. Add 3 tablespoons of the cheese and the herbs and stir together.

2 Beat together the egg and buttermilk in a separate bowl or jug. Use a knife or fork to combine the wet and dry ingredients lightly and bring them together to form a ball.

3 Shape the dough into a round, about 2.5 cm (1 inch) thick, and press out 12 rounds with a plain 5 cm (2 inch) cutter. Place the rounds on a lightly floured baking sheet and sprinkle over the reserved cheese.

4 Bake in a preheated oven, 220°C (425°F), Gas Mark 7, for 10-12 minutes until golden and well risen. The scones can be stored in an airtight container for up to 3 days.

Cheat's MEDITERRANEAN FOCACCIA

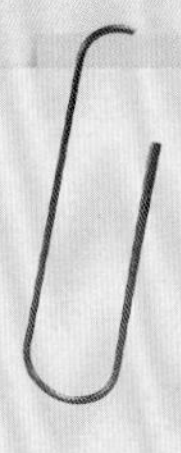

olive oil, for brushing
450 g (14½ oz) plain flour, plus extra for dusting
1 teaspoon bicarbonate of soda
1 teaspoon salt
1 tablespoon chopped rosemary, plus 10 small sprigs
100 g (3½ oz) sun-dried tomatoes, chopped
400 ml (14 fl oz) buttermilk
10 pitted black olives
1 teaspoon sea salt

Serves **8**
Prep time **15 minutes**
Cooking time **15 minutes**

1 Brush a 23 cm x 32 cm (9 inch x 12½ inch) Swiss roll tin generously with oil.

2 Sift the flour, bicarbonate of soda and salt into a large bowl. Stir in the chopped rosemary and sun-dried tomatoes. Make a well in the centre, add the buttermilk to the well and gradually stir into the flour. Bring the mixture together with your hands to form a soft, slightly sticky dough.

3 Tip the dough out on to a lightly floured surface and lightly knead for 1 minute, then quickly roll into a rectangular shape to fit the tin. Press the dough gently into the tin, then brush with oil. Using your finger, make small dimples in the top of the bread. Scatter over the black olives, rosemary sprigs and sea salt.

4 Bake in a preheated oven, 220°C (425°F), Gas Mark 7, for 15 minutes until brown and crisp. Brush with a little more olive oil and serve warm.

SPICED *Flatbreads*

1 Toast the cumin and coriander seeds in a dry frying pan over a medium heat until aromatic, then crush with a pestle and mortar. Alternatively, tip the cooled seeds into a plastic food bag and crush with the back of a spoon.

2 Mix together the flour, yeast, sugar, salt and toasted spices in a large bowl. Make a well in the centre, add the oil to the well and gradually stir into the flour with enough of 275 ml (9 fl oz) warm water to form a moist, pliable dough.

3 Tip the dough out on to a lightly floured surface and knead for 5 minutes until smooth and elastic. Divide into four balls and roll out thinly on a lightly floured surface into long oval or round shapes. Prick all over with a fork and arrange on nonstick baking sheets.

4 Bake in a preheated oven, 220°C (425°F), Gas Mark7, for 3 minutes. Turn the breads over and bake for a further 3 minutes until golden brown. Serve immediately or wrap in a clean tea towel or foil to keep warm before serving.

2 teaspoons cumin seeds
1 teaspoon coriander seeds
450 g (14½ oz) strong white flour, plus extra for dusting
7 g (¼ oz) sachet fast-action dried yeast
1 teaspoon caster sugar
1 teaspoon sea salt
1 tablespoon olive oil

Makes **4**
Prep time **15 minutes**
Cooking time **8 minutes**

Mixed Seed SODA BREAD

vegetable oil, for greasing
350 g (11½ oz) wholemeal plain flour, plus extra for dusting and sprinkling
50 g (2 oz) sunflower seeds
2 tablespoons poppy seeds
1 teaspoon bicarbonate of soda
1 teaspoon salt
1 teaspoon caster sugar
300 ml (½ pint) buttermilk

Makes 1 small loaf
Prep time **10 minutes**
Cooking time **40–45 minutes**

1 Lightly oil a baking sheet. Mix the flour, sunflower seeds, poppy seeds, bicarbonate of soda, salt and sugar together in a bowl. Make a well in the centre, add the buttermilk and gradually work into the flour mixture to form a soft dough.

2 Turn the dough out on a lightly floured work surface and knead for 5 minutes. Shape into a flattish round. Transfer to the baking sheet. Using a sharp knife, cut a cross in the top of the bread. Sprinkle a little extra flour over the surface.

3 Bake in a preheated oven, 230°C (450°F), Gas Mark 8, for 15 minutes, then reduce the temperature to 200°C (400°F), Gas Mark 6, and bake for a further 25–30 minutes until risen and the loaf sounds hollow when tapped underneath. Leave to cool completely on a wire rack.

BLACKBERRY *Muffin Slice*

THIS CAKE IS BEST EATEN FRESHLY MADE, PREFERABLY SLIGHTLY WARM.

100 g (3½ oz) unsalted butter, melted, plus extra for greasing
175 ml (6 fl oz) milk
1 egg
250 g (8 oz) plain flour
2 teaspoons baking powder
150 g (5 oz) caster sugar, plus extra for dusting
25 g (1 oz) porridge oats
100 g (3½ oz) fresh blackberries

Serves 6–8
Prep time 10 minutes
Cooking time 50–60 minutes

1 Grease and line the base and sides of a 500 g (1 lb) loaf tin so that the paper comes about 1 cm (½ inch) above the rim of the tin. Grease the paper.

2 Beat together the butter, milk and egg in a bowl or jug. Sift the flour and baking powder into a separate bowl and stir in the sugar, oats and half the blackberries. Stir the wet ingredients into the dry ingredients until only just combined.

3 Turn the mixture into the tin and scatter with the remaining blackberries. Bake in a preheated oven, 180°C (350°F), Gas Mark 4, for 50–60 minutes or until well risen, golden and firm to the touch. Leave in the tin for 5 minutes, then transfer to a wire rack and sprinkle with a little extra sugar. Serve warm or cold.

COOKING TIP

Summer fruit bargains like strawberries and blackberries can be frozen and used later on when the season has passed and the prices have skyrocketed. To freeze berries, spread them out in a single layer on a baking sheet and lay flat in the freezer. Once frozen, transfer to freezer bags and they won't stick together.

Lemon DRIZZLE CAKE

225 g (7½ oz) unsalted butter, softened, plus extra for greasing
225 g (7½ oz) caster sugar
finely grated rind of 3 lemons, plus 100 ml (3½ fl oz) lemon juice
4 eggs, beaten
250 g (8 oz) self-raising flour
1 teaspoon baking powder
75 g (3 oz) ground almonds
100 g (3½ oz) granulated sugar

Serves **8–10**
Prep time **20 minutes**
Cooking time **45 minutes**

1 Grease and line the base and sides of a 20 cm (8 inch) round cake tin or an 18 cm (7 inch) square tin. Grease the paper.

2 Beat together the butter, caster sugar and lemon rind in a bowl until light and fluffy. Beat in the eggs, a little at a time, beating well between each addition. Add a little of the flour if the mixture starts to curdle.

3 Sift the flour and baking powder into the bowl, add the ground almonds and 2 tablespoons of the lemon juice and gently fold in using a large metal spoon.

4 Turn the mixture into the tin and level the surface. Bake in a preheated oven, 180°C (350°F), Gas Mark 4, for about 45 minutes or until just firm and a skewer inserted into the centre comes out clean.

5 Meanwhile, mix together the remaining lemon juice with the granulated sugar. Transfer the cake to a wire rack. Give the lemon mixture a good stir and spoon it over the cake. As the cake cools the syrup will sink into the cake, leaving a sugary crust.

Victoria
SANDWICH CAKE

SANDWICH WITH JAM FOR A CLASSIC VICTORIA SPONGE OR, FOR A MORE DECADENT FILLING, SPREAD WITH JAM AND 150 ML (1/4 PINT) WHIPPED DOUBLE CREAM.

175 g (6 oz) unsalted butter, softened, plus extra for greasing
175 g (6 oz) caster sugar
3 eggs, beaten
175 g (6 oz) self-raising flour
5 tablespoons strawberry or raspberry jam
icing sugar or Buttercream (see page 251)

Serves **8**
Prep time **20 minutes**
Cooking time **25 minutes**

1 Grease and line the bases of two 18 cm (7 inch) round sandwich tins.

2 Beat together the butter and sugar in a bowl until very pale in colour, light and fluffy. Beat in the eggs, a little at a time, beating well after each addition. Add a little of the flour if the mixture starts to curdle.

3 Sift the flour into the bowl and gently fold in, using a large metal spoon. Don't beat it or overmix or you will knock out all the air.

4 Divide the mixture between the tins and level the surface. Bake in a preheated oven, 180°C (350°F), Gas Mark 4, for about 25 minutes or until risen and just firm to the touch. Loosen the edges of the sponges and turn out on to a wire rack to cool.

5 Sandwich the cakes together with the jam and sprinkle generously with icing sugar or spread with buttercream.

Vegan Banana Pecan Cake

V

WITH CARAMEL TOPPING

1 Lightly oil and line a loaf tin with a base measurement of about 18 x 9 cm (7 x 3¾ inches). Lightly oil the paper.

2 Mash the bananas in a bowl and stir in the oil until evenly combined. Sift the flour, baking powder and cinnamon into the bowl and add the sugar, nuts and dried fruit.

3 Stir the ingredients together until well mixed and turn into the tin. Bake in a preheated oven, 180°C (350°F), Gas Mark 4, for 30 minutes until slightly risen and just firm to the touch. Transfer to a wire rack to cool.

4 For the topping, put half the milk in a saucepan with the sugar and heat until the sugar dissolves. Bring to the boil and boil for 4–5 minutes until the syrup starts to turn golden around the edges. Meanwhile, blend the cornflour into the remaining milk and mix until smooth. Add to the saucepan and cook, stirring, for 2–3 minutes until thickened. Leave to cool before spreading over the cake and scattering with extra nuts.

3 tablespoons vegetable oil, plus extra for greasing
2 small very ripe bananas
125 g (4 oz) self-raising flour
½ teaspoon baking powder
½ teaspoon ground cinnamon
50 g (2 oz) light muscovado sugar
50 g (2 oz) pecan nuts, chopped, plus extra to decorate
25 g (1 oz) sultanas or raisins

Caramel topping
100 ml (3½ fl oz) unsweetened almond milk
50 g (2 oz) caster sugar
1 teaspoon cornflour

Serves **6**
Prep time **15 minutes, plus cooling**
Cooking time **40 minutes**

CHOCOLATE Fudge Cake

THIS IS A RICH, CHOCOLATE-PACKED CAKE WITH NOT THE FAINTEST HINT OF DRYNESS.

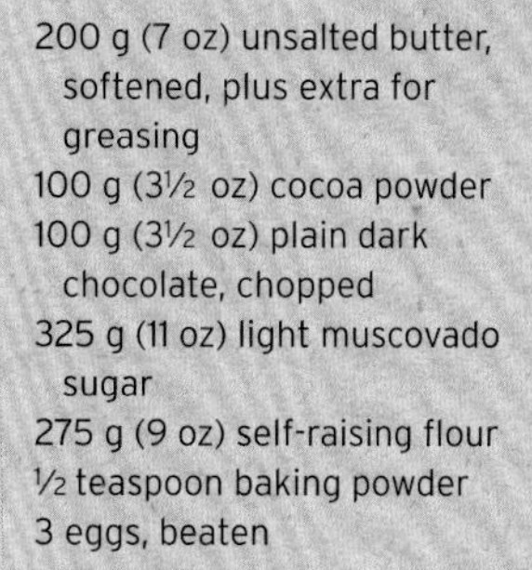

200 g (7 oz) unsalted butter, softened, plus extra for greasing
100 g (3½ oz) cocoa powder
100 g (3½ oz) plain dark chocolate, chopped
325 g (11 oz) light muscovado sugar
275 g (9 oz) self-raising flour
½ teaspoon baking powder
3 eggs, beaten

Fudge icing
300 g (10 oz) plain dark chocolate, broken up
225 g (7½ oz) icing sugar
200 g (7 oz) unsalted butter, softened

Serves **12**
Prep time **25 minutes, plus cooling**
Cooking time **20–25 minutes**

1 Grease and line the bases of three 20 cm (8 inch) sandwich tins. (If you only have two tins, bake a third of the cake mix afterwards.)

2 Whisk the cocoa powder in a bowl with 300 ml (½ pint) boiling water until smooth. Stir in the chopped chocolate and leave to cool, stirring occasionally.

3 Beat together the butter, sugar, flour, baking powder and eggs in a bowl until smooth. Beat in the chocolate mixture.

4 Divide the mixture evenly among the tins and level the surface. Bake in a preheated oven, 180°C (350°F), Gas Mark 4, for 20–25 minutes or until just firm to the touch. Transfer to a wire rack to cool.

5 Make the icing. Melt the chocolate in a small heatproof bowl set over a pan of simmering water (do not let the bowl touch the water). Remove from the heat and leave to cool slightly. Beat the icing sugar and butter together until creamy, then beat in the chocolate until smooth. Use the icing to sandwich the cake layers on a serving plate. Pile the remainder on top, spreading it evenly with a palette knife over the cake.

LEMON POPPING *Candy Cakes*

125 g (4 oz) unsalted butter, softened, plus extra for greasing
125 g (4 oz) caster sugar
125 g (4 oz) self-raising flour
2 eggs
1 tablespoon milk
2 teaspoons finely grated lemon rind
150 g (5 oz) icing sugar, sifted
about 2 teaspoons lemon juice
popping candy, to sprinkle

Makes **12**
Prep time **15 minutes, plus cooling**
Cooking time **12–15 minutes**

1 Line a 12-hole muffin tin with paper cases or lightly grease the holes.

2 Beat together the butter, sugar, flour, eggs, milk and 1 teaspoon of the lemon rind in a bowl until pale and creamy.

3 Divide the mixture among the cases or holes of the muffin tin and bake in a preheated oven, 190°C (375°F), Gas Mark 5, for 12–15 minutes until golden and risen. Transfer to a wire rack to cool.

4 Meanwhile, mix the icing sugar with the remaining lemon rind and just enough lemon juice to create a very thick, smooth icing. Spread over the cold cupcakes and sprinkle with popping candy.

VEGAN CHILLI & LIME Chocolate Muffins

V

1 Line a muffin tin with 10 paper muffin cases.

2 Sift the flour, chilli powder and cocoa powder into a bowl. Stir in the sugar and salt. Mix together the lime rind, vegetable oil, milk and vanilla extract in a separate bowl or jug. Add to the dry ingredients and stir together until combined.

3 Spoon the mixture into the muffin cases so they're almost full. Bake in a preheated oven, 190°C (375°F), Gas Mark 5, for 20 minutes until risen and just firm to the touch. Turn off the oven and leave the muffins to cool in the oven.

4 For the glaze, put the sugar, cocoa powder, lime juice and 2 tablespoons water in a small saucepan and heat gently until the sugar dissolves. Bring to the boil and boil for 30–60 seconds until slightly thickened. Drizzle over the muffins.

200 g (7 oz) self-raising flour
¼ teaspoon chilli powder
75 g (3 oz) cocoa powder
200 g (7 oz) light muscovado sugar
good pinch of salt
finely grated rind of 2 limes
150 ml (¼ pint) vegetable oil
100 ml (3½ fl oz) unsweetened almond milk or soya milk
1 teaspoon vanilla extract

Glaze
2 tablespoons light brown sugar
1 tablespoon cocoa powder
1 tablespoon lime juice

Makes **10**
Prep time **15 minutes, plus cooling**
Cooking time **25 minutes**

Chocolate MOCHA BROWNIES

LIKE ALL THE BEST BROWNIE RECIPES, THIS VERSION'S BOTH GOOEY AND FUDGY. TRY TO RESIST THE TEMPTATION TO OVER-INDULGE – THEY ARE PACKED WITH CHOCOLATE AND INCREDIBLY RICH!

175 g (6 oz) unsalted butter, plus extra for greasing
250 g (8 oz) plain dark chocolate, broken up
2 tablespoons instant coffee
3 eggs
225 g (7½ oz) light muscovado sugar
75 g (3 oz) self-raising flour
½ teaspoon baking powder
200 g (7 oz) milk chocolate, roughly chopped

1 Grease and line a shallow 27 x 18 cm (11 x 7 inch) rectangular tin or a 23 cm (9 inch) square tin.

2 Melt the plain chocolate with the butter in a heatproof bowl set over a pan of simmering water (do not let the bowl touch the water), stirring frequently, until smooth. Stir in the coffee.

3 In a separate bowl, beat together the eggs and sugar. Stir in the melted chocolate mixture, sift the flour and baking powder into the bowl and stir until they are combined.

4 Add the chopped milk chocolate and turn the mixture into the tin. Level the surface and bake in a preheated oven, 190°C (375°F), Gas Mark 5, for about 30 minutes or until a crust has formed but the mixture feels quite soft underneath. Leave to cool in the tin, then cut into squares.

Makes **15**
Prep time **15 minutes**
Cooking time **30 minutes**

CHOCOLATE CHIP COOKIES

125 g (4 oz) unsalted butter, softened
175 g (6 oz) soft light brown sugar
1 teaspoon vanilla extract
1 egg, lightly beaten
1 tablespoon milk
200 g (7 oz) plain flour
1 teaspoon baking powder
250 g (8 oz) plain dark chocolate chips

Makes 16
Prep time 10 minutes
Cooking time 15 minutes

1 Line a large baking sheet with nonstick baking paper.

2 Beat the butter and sugar together in a large bowl until light and fluffy. Mix in the vanilla extract, then gradually beat in the egg, beating well after each addition. Stir in the milk.

3 Sift the flour and baking powder into a separate large bowl, then fold into the butter and egg mixture. Stir in the chocolate chips.

4 Drop level tablespoonfuls of the cookie mixture on to the baking sheet, leaving about 3.5 cm (1½ inches) between each cookie, then lightly press with a floured fork. Bake in a preheated oven, 180°C (350°F), Gas Mark 4, for 15 minutes or until lightly golden. Transfer to a wire rack to cool.

AFFORDABILITY 1

Chewy Oat & RAISIN BARS

1 Grease and line the base of a 25 (10 inch) square baking tin, with a depth of about 3.5 cm (1½ inches).

2 Melt the butter with the golden syrup or honey, the condensed milk and sugar in a large pan over a medium-low heat, then remove from the heat and stir in the oats, raisins and flour. Stir well.

3 Scrape the mixture into the tin and bake in a preheated oven, 180°C (350°F), Gas Mark 4, for 15–18 minutes until pale golden in colour. Leave to cool in the tin for 2–3 minutes.

4 Cut about 16 squares or bars, then leave to cool in the tin for 5 minutes or until cool and firm enough to handle. Transfer to a wire rack.

200 g (7 oz) unsalted butter, plus extra for greasing
75 g (3 oz) golden syrup or clear honey
150 g (5 oz) sweetened condensed milk
125 g (4 oz) granulated sugar
325 g (11 oz) rolled oats
75 g (3 oz) raisins
75 g (3 oz) self-raising flour

Makes **16**
Prep time **5 minutes**
Cooking time **18–20 minutes**

CRUMBLY RASPBERRY & OAT SLICES

175 g (6 oz) unsalted butter, slightly softened and diced, plus extra for greasing
100 g (3½ oz) plain flour
75 g (3 oz) plain wholemeal flour
175 g (6 oz) porridge oats
150 g (5 oz) golden caster sugar
finely grated rind of 1 lemon
250 g (8 oz) fresh or frozen raspberries
icing sugar, for dusting

Makes **12-14**
Prep time **15 minutes**
Cooking time **1 hour**

1 Lightly grease the base and sides of a shallow 27 x 18 cm (10½ x 7 inch) rectangular baking tin or a similar-sized roasting tin.

2 Place the flours and oats in a bowl, add the butter and rub in with the fingertips until the mixture resembles coarse breadcrumbs. Stir in the sugar and lemon rind and continue to crumble the mixture together until it starts to cling together.

3 Turn half the mixture into the tin and pat it down into an even layer. Scatter the raspberries on top and sprinkle with the remaining crumble mixture.

4 Bake in a preheated oven, 180°C (350°F), Gas Mark 4, for about 1 hour or until the topping is turning golden. Cut into fingers and leave to cool in the tin. Serve dusted with icing sugar.

CRANBERRY, OATMEAL & CINNAMON SCONES

LIKE ALL SCONES, THESE SWEET FRUIT-SPECKED ONES ARE BEST SERVED FRESHLY BAKED, OR FROZEN AHEAD AND THEN WARMED THROUGH TO SERVE.

75 g (3 oz) unsalted butter, diced, plus extra for greasing
175 g (6 oz) self-raising flour, plus extra for dusting
1 teaspoon baking powder
1 teaspoon ground cinnamon
75 g (3 oz) caster sugar
50 g (2 oz) oatmeal, plus extra for sprinkling
75 g (3 oz) dried cranberries
5–6 tablespoons milk
beaten egg or milk, to glaze

Makes **10**
Prep time **10 minutes**
Cooking time **10–12 minutes**

1 Grease a baking sheet.

2 Place the flour, baking powder and cinnamon in a bowl, add the butter and rub in with the fingertips until the mixture resembles breadcrumbs. Stir in the sugar and oatmeal. Add the cranberries and milk and stir briefly until the mixture forms a soft dough, adding a little more milk if necessary.

3 Turn out on to a floured surface and roll out to 1.5 cm (¾ inch) thick. Cut out rounds using a 5 cm (2 inch) cutter. Transfer to the baking sheet and re-roll the trimmings to make 10 scones.

4 Brush with beaten egg or milk and sprinkle with oatmeal. Bake in a preheated oven, 220°C (425°F), Gas Mark 7, for 10–12 minutes until risen and golden. Transfer to a wire rack to cool. Serve split and buttered.

108 SWEETCORN CAKES WITH AVOCADO SALSA

110 TRICOLORE AVOCADO & COUSCOUS SALAD

111 BULGAR WHEAT WITH GOATS' CHEESE & RED ONION

112 CORN & BEAN TORTILLA STACK

114 FALAFEL CAKES

115 NUT KOFTAS WITH MINTED YOGURT

116 RICOTTA & BROAD BEAN FRITTERS

117 COUSCOUS FRITTERS WITH BEETROOT

118 GRIDDLED GREEK-STYLE SANDWICHES

120 SMOKEY BEAN & CHEESE BURGERS

121 CHEDDAR BURGERS WITH CUCUMBER SALSA

122 SPRING ONION, DILL & CHIVE PANCAKES

123 SPINACH & POTATO TORTILLA

124 HALOUMI WITH POMEGRANATE SALSA

126 FIVE-MINUTE PAD THAI

127 GINGERY GRILLED TOFU WITH NOODLES

STIR-FRIED TOFU

128 STIR-FRIED TOFU WITH BASIL & CHILLI

129 SPINACH & MUSHROOM RAMEN

130 THAI GREEN VEGETABLE CURRY

131 MANGO CURRY

132 CREAMY COURGETTE ORZO PASTA

134 KALE & PESTO LINGUINE

135 SPAGHETTI WITH GARLIC & BLACK PEPPER

138 FLASH-IN-THE-PAN RATATOUILLE

139 MIXED BEAN KEDGEREE

140 GARLIC & PAPRIKA SOUP WITH A FLOATING EGG

141 AUBERGINE PÂTÉ

Made in a Flash

KALE & PESTO LINGUINE

MANGO CURRY

SWEETCORN CAKES WITH AVOCADO SALSA

1 Place three-quarters of the sweetcorn kernels along with the spring onions, eggs, coriander, flour and baking powder in a food processor and whizz until combined. Alternatively, whizz the ingredients in batches using a stick blender. Season well and transfer to a large bowl. Add the remaining sweetcorn kernels and mix well.

2 Heat 1 tablespoon of the oil in a large nonstick frying pan over a medium-high heat. When the oil is hot, drop heaped tablespoons of the mixture into the pan and cook for 1 minute on each side. Drain on kitchen paper and keep warm in a low oven while cooking the remaining mixture in the same way.

3 To make the avocado salsa, place all the ingredients in a bowl and stir very gently to combine. Serve the warm sweetcorn cakes garnished with coriander leaves, with the tangy avocado salsa.

500 g (1 lb) fresh sweetcorn kernels
4 spring onions, finely sliced
2 eggs
5 tablespoons finely chopped coriander leaves, plus extra to garnish
125 g (4 oz) plain flour
1 teaspoon baking powder
salt and pepper
vegetable oil, for frying

Avocado salsa
2 ripe avocados, peeled, stoned and finely diced
4 tablespoons each of chopped mint and coriander leaves
2 tablespoons lime juice
2 tablespoons finely chopped red onion
½ teaspoon Tabasco sauce

Serves **4**
Prep time **15 minutes**
Cooking time **10 minutes**

Tricolore AVOCADO & COUSCOUS Salad

200 g (7 oz) couscous
300 ml (½ pint) hot Vegetable Stock (see page 246) or boiling water
250 g (8 oz) cherry tomatoes
2 avocados, peeled, stoned and chopped
150 g (5 oz) mozzarella cheese, chopped
handful of rocket leaves

Dressing
2 tablespoons homemade (see page 249) or ready-made pesto
1 tablespoon lemon juice
4 tablespoons olive oil
salt and pepper

Serves **4**
Prep time **10 minutes, plus standing**

1 Mix the couscous and stock or water together in a bowl, then cover with a plate and leave to stand for 10 minutes.

2 To make the dressing, mix the pesto with the lemon juice and season, then gradually mix in the oil. Pour over the couscous and mix with a fork.

3 Add the tomatoes, avocados and mozzarella to the couscous, mix well, then lightly stir in the rocket.

Bulgar Wheat
WITH GOATS' CHEESE & RED ONION

- 750 ml (1¼ pints) hot Vegetable Stock (see page 246)
- 275 g (9 oz) bulgar wheat
- 4 tablespoons vegetable oil
- 1 large red onion, halved and thinly sliced
- 100 ml (3½ fl oz) tomato juice
- 2 tablespoons lime juice
- 175 g (6 oz) firm goats' cheese, crumbled
- 3 tablespoons roughly chopped flat leaf parsley
- salt and pepper

Serves **4**
Prep time **10 minutes**
Cooking time **15 minutes**

1 Bring the stock to the boil in a large saucepan, add the bulgar wheat and cook for 7 minutes. Remove from the heat, cover with a tight-fitting lid and set aside for 5–8 minutes until the liquid has been absorbed and the grains are tender.

2 Meanwhile, heat 2 tablespoons of oil in a frying pan, add the onion and cook gently for 7-8 minutes until soft and golden.

3 Combine the remaining oil with the tomato juice and lime juice, then season with salt and pepper. Fold the dressing, onion, goats' cheese and parsley into the bulgar wheat with a fork, then spoon into warmed shallow bowls to serve.

CORN & BEAN TORTILLA STACK

1 Heat the oil in a large saucepan, add the chopped peppers, cover with a lid and cook gently for 5 minutes. Add the tomatoes, beans, sweetcorn and chilli powder. Bring to the boil and simmer, uncovered, for 7–8 minutes until the mixture is quite thick.

2 Place one tortilla on a baking sheet. Top with one-third of the bean mixture and one-quarter of the cheese. Repeat this twice to make three layers and then place the final tortilla on top. Sprinkle with the remaining cheese and bake in a preheated oven, 190°C (375°F), Gas Mark 5, for 15 minutes.

3 Garnish with the chopped coriander leaves and serve with avocado and soured cream, if liked.

2 tablespoons vegetable oil
2 red peppers, cored, deseeded and chopped
400 g (13 oz) can chopped tomatoes
2 x 400 g (13 oz) cans kidney beans, drained
2 x 200 g (7 oz) cans sweetcorn, drained
½ teaspoon chilli powder
4 large corn tortillas
200 g (7 oz) Cheddar cheese, grated
1 tablespoon finely chopped coriander leaves, to garnish

To serve
soured cream (optional)
1 avocado, peeled, stoned and sliced (optional)

Serves **4**
Prep time **15 minutes**
Cooking time **30 minutes**

FALAFEL CAKES

THESE TASTY CHICKPEA CAKES, TRADITIONALLY ROLLED INTO LITTLE BALLS AND DEEP-FRIED, MAKE A GREAT VEGGIE SUPPER SERVED SIMPLY WITH A FRESH, GREEK-STYLE SALAD.

400 g (13 oz) can chickpeas, rinsed and drained
1 onion, roughly chopped
3 garlic cloves, roughly chopped
2 teaspoons cumin seeds
1 teaspoon mild chilli powder
2 tablespoons chopped mint
3 tablespoons chopped fresh coriander
50 g (2 oz) fresh breadcrumbs
vegetable oil, for shallow-frying
salt and pepper

Serves **4**
Prep time **10 minutes**
Cooking time **10 minutes**

1 Using a stick blender, or a food processor or blender if you have one, briefly whizz the chickpeas with the onion, garlic, spices, herbs, breadcrumbs and a little salt and pepper to make a chunky paste.

2 Take dessertspoonfuls of the mixture and flatten into cakes. Heat a 1 cm (½ inch) depth of oil in a frying pan and fry half the falafel for about 3 minutes, turning once until crisp and golden. Drain on kitchen paper and keep warm while cooking the remainder in the same way.

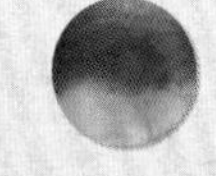

COOKING TIP

Don't throw away crusts of bread – blitz dry, stale bread in a food processor (try using a stick blender or a cheese grater if you don't have a processor) and keep in a sealed bag in the freezer. That way you always have a ready supply of breadcrumbs for crumble and pasta bake toppings and burger mixes.

NUT KOFTAS

with minted yogurt

5-6 tablespoons vegetable oil
1 onion, chopped
½ teaspoon dried chilli flakes
2 garlic cloves, roughly chopped
1 tablespoon medium curry paste (suitable for vegetarians)
425 g (14 oz) can borlotti or cannellini beans, rinsed and drained
125 g (4 oz) ground almonds
75 g (3 oz) chopped honey-roast or salted almonds
1 small egg
flour, for dusting
200 ml (7 fl oz) Greek yogurt
2 tablespoons chopped mint
1 tablespoon lemon juice
salt and pepper
warm naan bread, to serve
mint sprigs, to garnish

Serves 4
Prep time **15 minutes**
Cooking time **10 minutes**

1 Soak eight bamboo skewers in hot water while preparing the koftas. Alternatively, use metal skewers which do not require pre-soaking.

2 Heat 3 tablespoons of the oil in a frying pan, add the onion and fry for 4 minutes. Add the chilli flakes, garlic and curry paste and fry for 1 minute. Transfer to a food processor or blender with the beans, ground almonds, chopped almonds, egg and a little salt and pepper and process until the mixture starts to bind together. Alternatively, blend together in a bowl using a stick blender – you may need to do this in batches.

3 Using lightly floured hands, take about one-eighth of the mixture and mould around a skewer, forming it into a sausage about 2.5 cm (1 inch) thick. Make seven more koftas in the same way. Place on a foil-lined grill rack and brush with a further 1 tablespoon of the oil. Cook under a preheated medium grill for about 5 minutes, turning once, until golden.

4 Meanwhile, mix together the yogurt and mint in a small serving bowl and season to taste with salt and pepper. In a separate bowl, mix together the remaining oil, lemon juice and a little salt and pepper.

5 Brush the koftas with the lemon dressing and serve with the yogurt dressing on warm naan bread garnished with mint sprigs.

Ricotta & BROAD BEAN Fritters

1 Cook the broad beans in a saucepan of boiling water for 2 minutes to soften. Drain well and roughly chop.

2 Put the beans in a bowl and beat in the shallot, ricotta, egg yolk and capers. Stir in the flour and a little salt and pepper. Whisk the egg white in a thoroughly clean bowl until peaking. Gently stir the egg white into the bean mixture until just combined.

3 Mix together the ingredients for the dip and season lightly.

4 Heat a dash of oil in a frying pan. Place dessertspoonfuls of the batter in the pan and flatten slightly with the back of the spoon. Fry gently for 3–4 minutes, turning once, until golden. Drain on kitchen paper and keep warm while cooking the remainder in the same way. Serve with the dip and a leafy salad.

100 g (3½ oz) frozen baby broad beans
1 shallot, grated or finely chopped
125 g (4 oz) ricotta cheese
1 egg, separated
1 tablespoon capers, drained
50 g (2 oz) plain flour
vegetable oil, for frying
salt and pepper
leafy salad, to serve

Yogurt dip
4 tablespoons Greek yogurt
1 small garlic clove, crushed
2 tablespoons chopped mint
finely grated rind of ½ lemon

Serves **2**
Prep time **15 minutes**
Cooking time **10 minutes**

COUSCOUS FRITTERS WITH BEETROOT

150 g (5 oz) couscous
100 ml (3½ fl oz) hot Vegetable Stock (see page 246)
4 spring onions, finely chopped
2 garlic cloves, chopped
3 tablespoons chopped parsley, plus extra to garnish
75 g (3 oz) pine nuts, roughly chopped
50 g (2 oz) ground almonds
finely grated rind of 1 lemon
1 egg
vegetable oil, for frying
4 small cooked beetroots, cut into wedges
salt and pepper
crème fraîche, to serve

Dressing
4 tablespoons olive oil
1 teaspoon Tabasco sauce
1 tablespoon lemon juice

Serves **4**
Prep time **15 minutes**
Cooking time **5 minutes**

1 Place two-thirds of the couscous in a bowl, add the stock and leave to stand for 5 minutes. Meanwhile, mix together the ingredients for the dressing in a small bowl.

2 When the couscous has absorbed all the stock, fluff up with a fork and stir in the spring onions, garlic, parsley, pine nuts, almonds, lemon rind and egg. Season with salt and pepper and mix until the ingredients bind together.

3 Take heaped teaspoonfuls of the mixture and shape into balls. Roll them in the remaining couscous. Wet your hands before rolling the balls if the mixture starts to stick.

4 Heat a 2.5 cm (1 inch) depth of oil in a frying pan or heavy-based saucepan. Add half the couscous balls and fry for about 2 minutes until golden. Drain on kitchen paper and keep warm while cooking the remainder in the same way.

5 Arrange the beetroot wedges on warmed serving plates and pile the fritters beside them. Top with a spoonful of crème fraîche, garnish with parsley and serve with the dressing spooned over the top.

Griddled GREEK-STYLE SANDWICHES

1 Mix together the onion, tomatoes, olives, cucumber, oregano and feta in a small bowl. Add the lemon juice, season to taste with pepper and gently mix.

2 Split each pitta bread in half horizontally. Divide the feta mixture between the bottom halves of the pitta breads, then add the Cheddar. Cover with the top halves of the pitta breads.

3 Brush a frying pan with oil and heat over a medium heat. When hot, add the sandwiches, press down gently with a spatula and cook for 2–3 minutes on each side until golden and the cheese has melted. Serve immediately.

AFFORDABILITY 1

¼ small red onion, thinly sliced
8 cherry tomatoes, quartered
4 pitted black olives, chopped
5 cm (2 inch) piece of cucumber, deseeded and cut into small pieces
1 teaspoon dried oregano
50 g (2 oz) feta cheese, crumbled
1 teaspoon lemon juice
2 round seeded pitta breads
25 g (1 oz) Cheddar cheese, grated
olive oil, for brushing
pepper

Serves **2**
Prep time **15 minutes**
Cooking time **4–6 minutes**

Smokey Bean & Cheese BURGERS

400 g (13 oz) can black beans
1 small carrot, finely grated
2 spring onions, finely chopped
50 g (2 oz) fresh brown or white breadcrumbs
75 g (3 oz) Manchego or Cheddar cheese, grated
1 teaspoon smoked paprika
1 egg, beaten
2 tablespoons vegetable oil
salt

To serve
rocket leaves
burger buns, split
tomato slices
sliced green jalapeño chillies
mayonnaise

Serves 4
Prep time **15 minutes**
Cooking time **6–8 minutes**

1 Thoroughly drain the beans and pat dry between several sheets of kitchen paper. Transfer to a bowl and mash roughly with a fork. Add the carrot, spring onions, breadcrumbs, cheese, paprika and a little salt and stir well to combine. Add the egg and mix to a very thick paste.

2 Divide the mixture into four equal-sized pieces and shape each into a burger. Heat the oil in a frying pan and fry the burgers for 3–4 minutes on each side until browned and heated through.

3 Place handfuls of rocket leaves on the burger bases and position the burgers on top. Add tomato and chilli slices and mayonnaise, then top with the bun lids to serve.

CHEDDAR BURGERS WITH CUCUMBER SALSA

200 g (7 oz) can butter beans, rinsed and drained
1 onion, finely chopped
1 carrot, grated
100 g (3½ oz) mature Cheddar cheese, grated
100 g (3½ oz) fresh breadcrumbs
1 egg
1 teaspoon cumin seeds
flour, for dusting
vegetable oil, for shallow-frying
4 round French rolls
salt and pepper
salad, to serve

Salsa
½ small cucumber
2 tablespoons chopped fresh coriander
2 spring onions, finely chopped
1 tablespoon lemon or lime juice
1 teaspoon caster sugar

Serves **4**
Prep time **10 minutes**
Cooking time **8 minutes**

1 Place the butter beans in a bowl and lightly mash with a fork. Add the onion, carrot, cheese, breadcrumbs, egg, cumin seeds and salt and pepper and mix until evenly combined.

2 Using lightly floured hands, shape the mixture into four small flat cakes. Heat a little oil in a large frying pan and fry the burgers for about 8 minutes, turning once, until crisp and golden.

3 Meanwhile, make the salsa. Halve the cucumber and scoop out the seeds. Finely chop the cucumber and toss in a bowl with the coriander, spring onions, lemon or lime juice, sugar and a little salt and pepper.

4 Split the rolls and sandwich with the burgers and salsa. Serve with salad.

SPRING ONION, *Dill & Chive* PANCAKES

175 g (6 oz) plain flour
1 teaspoon baking powder
150 ml (1/4 pint) milk
2 large eggs
50 g (2 oz) butter, melted
2 tablespoons each of finely chopped dill and chives, plus extra to garnish
4 spring onions, finely chopped
vegetable oil, for shallow-frying
salt and pepper

To serve
200 g (7 oz) cream cheese, whisked with juice of 1 lemon
2 plum tomatoes, finely chopped

Serves **4**
Prep time **10 minutes**
Cooking time **20-35 minutes**

1 Sift the flour and baking powder into a bowl with a pinch of salt. Whisk together the milk, eggs, butter, herbs and spring onions in a separate bowl. Stir the wet mixture into the dry ingredients until the mixture comes together as a smooth, thick batter.

2 Heat a little vegetable oil in a small nonstick frying pan and spoon in one-eighth of the batter. Cook the pancake for 1-2 minutes or until bubbles form on the surface, then carefully turn it over and cook for a further 1-2 minutes or until golden brown on both sides. Transfer to a plate and keep warm while cooking the remainder in the same way to make eight pancakes.

3 Stack two pancakes on each warmed serving plate and spoon over a dollop of the cream cheese mixture. Top with the chopped tomatoes and serve garnished with a sprinkling of herbs and freshly ground black pepper.

Spinach & Potato TORTILLA

3 tablespoons vegetable oil
2 onions, finely chopped
250 g (8 oz) cooked potatoes, peeled and cut into 1 cm (½ inch) cubes
2 garlic cloves, finely chopped
200 g (7 oz) cooked spinach, drained thoroughly and roughly chopped
4 tablespoons finely chopped roasted red pepper
5 eggs
3–4 tablespoons grated Manchego cheese
salt and pepper

Serves 4
Prep time **15 minutes**
Cooking time **15–20 minutes**

1 Heat the oil in a flameproof nonstick frying pan, add the onions and potatoes and cook over a medium heat for 3–4 minutes or until the vegetables have softened but not coloured, turning and stirring frequently. Add the garlic, spinach and peppers and stir to mix well.

2 Beat the eggs lightly and season well. Pour into the frying pan, shaking the pan so that the egg is evenly spread. Cook gently for 8–10 minutes or until the tortilla is set at the bottom.

3 Sprinkle over the grated Manchego. Place the frying pan under a preheated medium-hot grill and cook for 3–4 minutes until the top is set and golden. Remove from the heat, cut into bite-sized squares or triangles and serve warm or at room temperature.

HALOUMI WITH POMEGRANATE SALSA

1 First make the pomegranate salsa. Carefully scoop the pomegranate seeds into a bowl, discarding all the white membrane. Stir in the remaining ingredients and season with salt and pepper.

2 Heat a large nonstick frying pan for 2–3 minutes until hot. Add the haloumi slices in batches and cook over a high heat for about 60 seconds on each side until browned and softened.

3 Meanwhile, warm the honey in a small saucepan until the honey is runny.

4 Transfer the pan-fried haloumi to warmed serving plates and spoon over the salsa. Drizzle the honey over the haloumi and salsa, then serve immediately.

500 g (1 lb) haloumi cheese, sliced
1 tablespoon clear honey

Pomegranate salsa
½ pomegranate
4 tablespoons olive oil
2 tablespoons chopped parsley
1 tablespoon lemon juice
1 small red chilli, deseeded and finely chopped
1 small garlic clove, crushed
1 teaspoon pomegranate syrup (optional)
salt and pepper

Serves **4**
Prep time **10 minutes**
Cooking time **10 minutes**

Five-Minute PAD THAI

V

1 Cook the noodles in a saucepan of boiling water for 3–4 minutes or until tender.

2 Meanwhile, heat the oil in a frying pan or wok, add the vegetables and cook for about 4 minutes, stirring frequently, until softened.

3 Mix together the soy sauce, peanut butter, lemon or lime juice, chilli flakes, sugar and 2 tablespoons water. Drain the noodles and add to the pan with the sauce and peanuts. Stir well to combine and serve hot.

100 g (3½ oz) dried ribbon rice noodles
1 tablespoon wok oil or stir-fry oil
300 g (10 oz) pack ready-prepared stir-fry vegetables with bean sprouts
2 tablespoons soy sauce
2 tablespoons crunchy peanut butter
1 tablespoon lemon or lime juice
¼ teaspoon dried chilli flakes
1 tablespoon light brown or caster sugar
40g (1½ oz) salted peanuts, roughly chopped

Serves **2**
Prep time **3 minutes**
Cooking time **5 minutes**

STUDENT TIP

Convenience stores are exactly that – fine for when you need an emergency pint of milk or a chocolate fix, but definitely not the place to head to when you're doing the weekly shop. You'll pay a premium for the convenience factor and should make a beeline for superstores if you want to stretch your budget.

GINGERY GRILLED TOFU *with* NOODLES

2 tablespoons vegetable oil
about 500 g (1 lb) ready-prepared stir-fry vegetables
400 g (13 oz) fresh noodles
400 g (13 oz) firm tofu, thickly sliced

Marinade
2.5 cm (1 inch) piece of fresh root ginger, peeled and grated
2 large garlic cloves, crushed
3 tablespoons dark soy sauce
3 tablespoons clear honey

Serves **4**
Prep time **5 minutes**
Cooking time **10 minutes**

1 Heat the oil in a frying pan or wok, add the vegetables and stir-fry for 3–4 minutes. Add the noodles and toss for a further 3–4 minutes.

2 Meanwhile, mix together the ginger, garlic, soy and honey. Add the sliced tofu and turn gently in the marinade to coat. Reserve the remaining marinade. Arrange the tofu on a foil-lined baking sheet and cook under a preheated medium grill for about 4 minutes, carefully turning once, until golden.

3 Remove the noodles from the heat, drizzle over the remaining marinade and serve topped with the grilled tofu.

Stir-Fried Tofu WITH BASIL & CHILLI

2 tablespoons vegetable oil
350 g (11½ oz) firm tofu, cubed
5 cm (2 inch) piece of fresh root ginger, peeled and grated
2 garlic cloves, chopped
250 g (8 oz) broccoli, trimmed
250 g (8 oz) sugar snap peas, trimmed
150 ml (¼ pint) Vegetable Stock (see page 246)
2 tablespoons sweet chilli sauce
1 tablespoon light soy sauce
1 tablespoon dark soy sauce
1 tablespoon lime juice
2 teaspoons soft light brown sugar
handful of Thai basil leaves
rice or noodles, to serve

Serves **4**
Prep time **20 minutes**
Cooking time **6 minutes**

1 Heat half the oil in a frying pan or wok until smoking, add the tofu and stir-fry for 2–3 minutes until golden all over. Remove with a slotted spoon.

2 Add the remaining oil to the pan, add the ginger and garlic and stir-fry for 10 seconds, then add the broccoli and sugar snap peas and stir-fry for 1 minute.

3 Return the tofu to the pan and add the stock, chilli sauce, soy sauces, lime juice and sugar. Cook for 1 minute until the vegetables are cooked but still crisp. Add the basil leaves and stir well. Serve immediately with rice or noodles.

SPINACH & MUSHROOM RAMEN

1 Heat the oil in a saucepan or wok, add the mushrooms and fry for 6–8 minutes until golden. Add the spring onions and garlic and cook for a further 1 minute.

2 Add the stock, chilli flakes and ginger and bring to a gentle simmer. Add the soy sauce, lemon juice and sugar, stirring in to mix. When heated through, add the spinach, stirring it through until wilted.

3 Meanwhile, cook the noodles in a saucepan of boiling water for 3 minutes or according to the pack directions until tender. Thoroughly drain the noodles into a warmed serving bowl and ladle the soup on top to serve.

AFFORDABILITY 1

1 tablespoon stir-fry oil or wok oil
125 g (4 oz) chestnut mushrooms, thinly sliced
½ bunch of spring onions, sliced diagonally
1 garlic clove, sliced
300 ml (½ pint) Vegetable Stock (see page 246)
good pinch of dried chilli flakes
1 cm (½ inch) piece of fresh root ginger, peeled and grated
1 tablespoon soy sauce
2 teaspoons lemon juice
1 teaspoon caster sugar
50 g (2 oz) spinach leaves, tough stalks removed
75 g (3 oz) Ramen noodles or egg noodles

Serves 1
Prep time 10 minutes
Cooking time 12 minutes

Thai Green Vegetable CURRY

- 2 red chillies (optional for hotter curry)
- 200 g (7 oz) carrots
- 250 g (8 oz) butternut squash
- 1 tablespoon vegetable oil
- 3 tablespoons Thai green curry paste (suitable for vegetarians)
- 400 ml (14 fl oz) can coconut milk
- 200 ml (7 fl oz) Vegetable Stock (see page 246)
- 6 kaffir lime leaves or 1 tablespoon finely grated lime rind
- 2 tablespoons soy sauce
- 1 tablespoon soft brown sugar
- 100 g (3½ oz) sugar snap peas
- 10 tablespoons very finely chopped coriander leaves
- juice of 1 lime
- steamed Jasmine rice, to serve

Serves **4**
Prep time **10 minutes**
Cooking time **12-16 minutes**

1 Deseed and finely slice the chillies, if using. Peel the carrots and cut into thick batons. Peel and deseed the butternut squash, then cut the flesh into 1.5 cm (¾ inch) cubes.

2 Heat the oil in a large nonstick wok or saucepan. Add the curry paste and chillies, if using, and stir-fry for 2–3 minutes.

3 Stir in the coconut milk, stock, lime leaves or lime rind, soy sauce, sugar, carrots and butternut squash. Simmer, uncovered, for 6–8 minutes, stirring occasionally.

4 Add the sugar snaps and continue to simmer for 4–5 minutes. Remove from the heat and stir in the coriander and lime juice. Serve with steamed Jasmine rice.

Mango CURRY

1 tablespoon vegetable oil
1 teaspoon mustard seeds
1 onion, thinly sliced
15–20 curry leaves, fresh or dried
½ teaspoon dried chilli flakes
1 teaspoon peeled and grated fresh root ginger
1 green chilli, deseeded and sliced
1 teaspoon turmeric
3 ripe mangoes, peeled, stoned and thinly sliced
400 ml (14 fl oz) natural yogurt, lightly beaten
salt
warm chapattis, to serve

Serves **4**
Prep time **10 minutes**
Cooking time **10 minutes**

1 Heat the oil in a large saucepan until hot, add the mustard seeds, onion, curry leaves and chilli flakes and fry, stirring, for 4–5 minutes or until the onion is lightly browned.

2 Add the ginger and chilli and stir-fry for 1 minute, then add the turmeric and stir to mix well.

3 Remove the pan from the heat, add the mangoes and yogurt and stir constantly until well mixed. Season to taste with salt.

4 Return the pan to a low heat and heat through for 1 minute, stirring constantly. (Do not let it boil or the curry will curdle.) Serve immediately with warm chapattis.

CREAMY Courgette ORZO PASTA

1 Heat the butter and oil in a large frying pan, add the chilli, garlic, spring onions and courgettes and cook over a medium-low heat for 10–15 minutes, stirring frequently, until softened.

2 Reduce the heat and add the lemon rind. Cook gently for 3–4 minutes, add the soft cheese and mix thoroughly. Season to taste.

3 Meanwhile, cook the pasta in a large saucepan of lightly salted boiling water according to the pack instructions until just tender.

4 Drain the pasta and add to the courgette mixture. Stir in the parsley, mix well and serve immediately.

1 tablespoon butter
1 tablespoon olive oil
1 red chilli, deseeded and finely chopped
2 garlic cloves, finely chopped
4 spring onions, very finely chopped
3 courgettes, coarsely grated
finely grated rind of 1 small lemon
150 g (5 oz) soft cheese with garlic and herbs
375 g (12 oz) dried orzo (rice-shaped pasta)
4 tablespoons finely chopped flat leaf parsley
salt and pepper

Serves **4**
Prep time **10 minutes**
Cooking time **15-20 minutes**

KALE & PESTO *Linguine*

375 g (12 oz) dried linguine
2 tablespoons olive oil
3 garlic cloves, crushed
300 g (10 oz) kale, tough stalks removed, roughly chopped
100 g (3½ oz) toasted pine nuts
100 g (3½ oz) mascarpone cheese
100 g (3½ oz) Pecorino-style cheese, grated, plus extra shavings to garnish
½ teaspoon grated nutmeg
salt and pepper

Serves **4**
Prep time **10 minutes**
Cooking time **10-12 minutes**

1 Cook the pasta in a large saucepan of lightly salted boiling water according to the pack instructions until just tender.

2 Meanwhile, heat the oil in a frying pan, add the garlic and fry for 2-3 minutes. Add the kale to the pan. Cover with a lid and cook for 2-3 minutes or until the kale starts to wilt.

3 Using a stick blender, or a food processor or blender if you have one, whizz the pine nuts until smooth. Tip in the mascarpone, cheese and nutmeg. Whizz again. Add the kale and garlic mixture and whizz until smooth. (If using a stick blender, you may need to do this in batches.) Season to taste.

4 Drain the pasta and return it to the pan. Add the pesto and toss to mix well. Serve with shavings of cheese.

SPAGHETTI
WITH GARLIC & BLACK PEPPER

200 g (7 oz) quick-cook spaghetti
3 tablespoons olive oil
2 garlic cloves, chopped
2 tablespoons lemon juice
pepper
grated Parmesan-style cheese, to serve

Serves 2
Prep time 5 minutes
Cooking time 3-5 minutes

1 Cook the spaghetti in a large saucepan of lightly salted boiling water for 3–5 minutes or according to the pack instructions until just tender.

2 Meanwhile, heat the oil in a frying pan with the garlic and warm gently for 2–3 minutes until softened but not coloured.

3 Drain the spaghetti and return to the pan, reserving 3 tablespoons of the cooking water. Pour over the garlic oil and stir in the reserved cooking liquid and lemon juice. Season with pepper and serve with grated cheese.

PACKING A *Lunch Punch*

One quick and easy way to stretch your weekly budget is to take your own lunch and snacks into college. While late nights and lazy lie-ins mean it's tempting to grab breakfast or lunch from the canteen, every egg muffin and baked potato is eating into cash reserves that could be better spent on other things.

BOXING CLEVER

There's nothing worse than unwrapping a soggy sandwich at lunchtime so it's worth investing in a couple of decent containers. If you're planning to get more creative than encasing a wedge of cheese between two slices of white bread, you can find lots of clever boxes with compartments, folding cutlery and separate sections for wet and dry ingredients. You might also want to buy a food flask for hot meals and an insulated lunch bag to keep food cool in the summer. Get into the habit of emptying and cleaning your lunch container as soon as you get home: you're more likely to make a packed lunch again the next day if you don't have to face smelly food scraps first thing in the morning.

SNACK ATTACK

It's not just canteen meals that can break the budget; coffees and mid-morning snacks all add up too. It's a good idea to tuck some fruit, nuts, granola bars or homemade biscuits in your bag for a quick energy boost during the day.

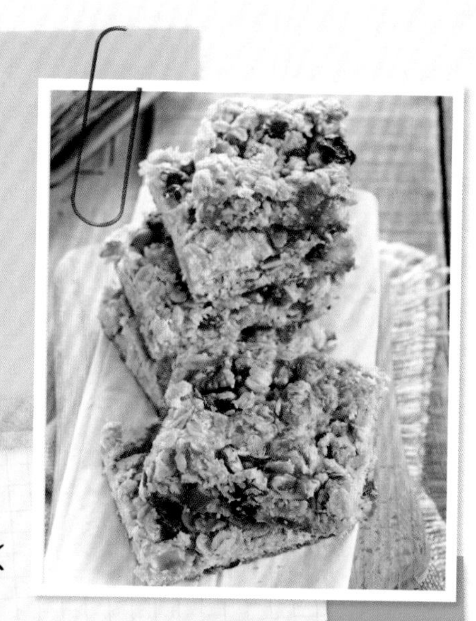

10 EASY LUNCHBOX IDEAS

1. Couscous salad – soak a handful of couscous in hot water for 15 minutes, then add chopped cucumber, red pepper, onion, celery and herbs, and some drained chickpeas or kidney beans.

2. Fill a pitta or wrap with grated carrot, cheese and hummus.

3. Treat yourself to a food flask and enjoy a hot meal of soup or leftover pasta.

4. Fill a sealable plastic container with sliced carrots, celery and cucumber and add a mini pot of hummus.

5. Put layers of natural yogurt, muesli, chopped fruit and honey in a sealable plastic container – don't forget a spoon.

6. Cold, roasted new potatoes make a great snack between lectures.

7. Cooked and cooled pasta can be mixed with pesto, cherry tomatoes and chopped cucumber for a filling lunch.

8. Add a quartered boiled egg to a mixed green salad for a protein hit.

9. Make a hearty potato and vegetable frittata for dinner and enjoy the leftovers for lunch the next day.

10. Put your favourite filling between two slices of bread and enjoy a good, old-fashioned sandwich.

FLASH-IN-THE-PAN Ratatouille

100 ml (3½ fl oz) olive oil
2 onions, chopped
1 aubergine, cut into 1.5 cm (¾ inch) cubes
2 large courgettes, cut into 1.5 cm (¾ inch) cubes
1 red pepper, cored, deseeded and cut into 1.5 cm (¾ inch) pieces
1 yellow pepper, cored, deseeded and cut into 1.5 cm (¾ inch) pieces
2 garlic cloves, crushed
400 g (13 oz) can chopped tomatoes
2–3 tablespoons balsamic vinegar
1 teaspoon soft brown sugar
10–12 pitted black olives
salt and pepper
torn basil leaves, to garnish

Serves **4**
Prep time **10 minutes**
Cooking time **20 minutes**

1 Heat the oil in a large pan until very hot, add all of the vegetables, except the tomatoes, and stir-fry for a few minutes.

2 Add the tomatoes, balsamic vinegar and sugar, season and stir well. Cover with a tight-fitting lid and simmer for 15 minutes until the vegetables are cooked.

3 Remove from the heat, scatter over the olives and torn basil leaves and serve.

MIXED BEAN KEDGEREE

1 Put the eggs in a saucepan of cold water and bring to the boil. Cook for 10 minutes, then plunge into cold water to cool. Shell the eggs, cut into wedges and set aside.

2 Meanwhile, heat the oil in a saucepan, add the onion and fry for about 3–4 minutes, until soft. Stir in the curry powder and rice, then add the stock. Bring to the boil, cover with a lid and simmer for 10–15 minutes until the rice is cooked.

3 Stir through the beans and soured cream. Season to taste, top with the eggs and serve garnished with the tomatoes and herbs.

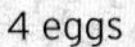

- 4 eggs
- 2 tablespoons vegetable oil
- 1 onion, chopped
- 2 tablespoons mild curry powder
- 250 g (8 oz) long grain rice
- 750 ml (1¼ pints) Vegetable Stock (see page 246)
- 2 x 400 g (13 oz) cans mixed beans, rinsed and drained
- 150 ml (¼ pint) soured cream
- salt and pepper

To garnish

- 2 tomatoes, finely chopped
- 3 tablespoons chopped fresh herbs

Serves **4**
Prep time **10 minutes**
Cooking time **15–20 minutes**

GARLIC & PAPRIKA SOUP
WITH A FLOATING EGG

4 tablespoons olive oil
12 thick slices of baguette
5 garlic cloves, sliced
1 onion, finely chopped
1 tablespoon paprika
1 teaspoon ground cumin
good pinch of saffron threads
1.2 litres (2 pints) Vegetable Stock (see page 246)
25 g (1 oz) dried soup pasta
4 eggs
salt and pepper

Serves 4
Prep time 5 minutes
Cooking time 20 minutes

1 Heat the oil in a heavy-based saucepan, add the bread and fry gently, turning once, until golden. Drain on kitchen paper.

2 Add the garlic, onion, paprika and cumin to the pan and fry gently for 3 minutes. Add the saffron and stock and bring to the boil. Stir in the soup pasta. Reduce the heat, cover with a lid and simmer for about 8 minutes until the pasta is just tender. Season to taste with salt and pepper.

3 Break the eggs on to a saucer and slide into the pan one at a time. Cook for about 2 minutes until poached.

4 Stack three fried bread slices in each soup bowl. Ladle the soup over the bread, making sure each serving contains an egg. Serve immediately.

Aubergine PÂTÉ

V

AFFORDABILITY 1

JUST A FEW DRIED MUSHROOMS REALLY BOOST THE FLAVOUR OF THIS QUICK AND EASY PÂTÉ. IT MAKES PLENTY AND LEFTOVERS KEEP WELL IN THE FRIDGE FOR SEVERAL DAYS, READY FOR EITHER ZIPPING UP VEGETABLE STEWS OR SPREADING ON TO TOAST AND GRILLING WITH GRUYÈRE CHEESE.

25 g (1 oz) dried porcini mushrooms
500 g (1 lb) aubergines
6 tablespoons olive oil
1 small red onion, chopped
2 teaspoons cumin seeds
175 g (6 oz) cup or chestnut mushrooms
2 garlic cloves, crushed
3 pickled walnuts, halved
small handful of fresh coriander
salt and pepper
toasted walnut or grainy bread, to serve

Serves **6**
Prep time **10 minutes, plus soaking**
Cooking time **15 minutes**

1 Place the dried mushrooms in a bowl and cover with plenty of boiling water. Leave to soak for 10 minutes.

2 Meanwhile, cut the aubergines into 1 cm (½ inch) dice. Heat the oil in a large frying pan, add the aubergines and onion and fry gently for 8 minutes until the vegetables are softened and browned.

3 Drain the dried mushrooms and add to the pan with the cumin seeds, fresh mushrooms and garlic. Fry for a further 5–7 minutes until the aubergines are very soft.

4 Transfer to a food processor or blender with the pickled walnuts and coriander, season to taste with salt and pepper and process until broken up but not completely smooth. Alternatively, whizz the ingredients in a bowl using a stick blender. Transfer to a serving dish and serve warm or cold with toast.

All the Carbs

CORGETTE & CREAMY TOMATO PENNE

SWISS CHEESE MELTS

144 GOATS' CHEESE & PEPPER LASAGNE

146 MUSHROOM, COURGETTE & MASCARPONE LASAGNE

147 VEGGIE CARBONARA

148 HALOUMI & ROCKET CARBONARA

149 AUBERGINE CANNELLONI

150 MUSHROOM TAGLIATELLE WITH GREMOLATA

152 COURGETTE & CREAMY TOMATO PENNE

153 TAGLIATELLE WITH BLUE CHEESE BUTTER

154 CREAMY MUSHROOM & TARRAGON RIGATONI

155 RIBBON PASTA WITH AUBERGINES & PINE NUTS

156 GOATS' CHEESE LINGUINE WITH GARLIC & HERB BUTTER

158 PASTA WITH FENNEL & ROCKET

159 MACARONI CHEESE WITH SPINACH

160 MUSHROOM, EGG & CRESS ALL-DAY PIZZA

161 SWISS CHEESE MELTS

162 SPICY MEXICAN WRAPS

163 TORTILLAS WITH MINTED CHILLI & AUBERGINE YOGURT

164 CAMEMBERT WRAPS WITH HOT PEPPER SALSA

165 RICE PILAF WITH KALE CRISPS

166 CREAMY MUSHROOM & CHIVE RISOTTO

168 EASY PEA RISOTTO

169 BEETROOT RISOTTO WITH HORSERADISH & MIXED LEAVES

170 LEMON & HERB RISOTTO

171 SAGE & TOMATO PILAF

172 CARROT & FETA POTATO CAKES

174 WARM MUSHROOMS WITH POTATO ROSTI

175 CHIMICHURRI CHIPS & BEANS

176 JAMAICAN COCONUT CURRY

177 VEGETABLE NOODLES IN SPICED COCONUT MILK

180 HOT & SPICY VEGETABLE NOODLES

181 BLACK BEAN SOUP WITH SOBA NOODLES

182 RICE NOODLE PANCAKES WITH STIR-FRIED VEGETABLES

SPINACH & POTATO GRATIN

GOATS' CHEESE & PEPPER LASAGNE

50 g (2 oz) dried porcini mushrooms
225 g (7½ oz) spinach leaves, tough stalks removed
4 tablespoons olive oil
1 large onion, sliced
2 red peppers, cored, deseeded and roughly chopped
3 garlic cloves, sliced
2 x 400 g (13 oz) cans chopped tomatoes
4 tablespoons homemade (see page 249) or ready-made red pesto
2 tablespoons chopped oregano
300 g (10 oz) soft goats' cheese
2 quantities Béchamel Sauce (see page 247)
200 g (7 oz) dried lasagne sheets
50 g (2 oz) fresh breadcrumbs
salt and pepper

Serves **4–5**
Prep time **30 minutes, plus soaking**
Cooking time **1 hour**

1 Put the mushrooms in a bowl, cover with 200 ml (7 fl oz) boiling water and leave to soak. Steam the spinach for 1-2 minutes until just wilted.

2 Heat 2 tablespoons of the oil in a saucepan, add the onion and peppers and fry for 5 minutes. Add the garlic, tomatoes, pesto, oregano, spinach, mushrooms and their soaking liquid and salt and pepper. Bring to the boil and simmer gently for 10 minutes.

3 Beat the goats' cheese into the béchamel sauce. Spoon one-quarter of the vegetable sauce into a shallow, 1.5 litre (2 ¾ pint) ovenproof dish. Spread with one-quarter of the béchamel sauce. Arrange one-third of the pasta sheets over the sauce, trimming or breaking them to fit.

4 Repeat the layering, finishing with béchamel sauce. Toss the breadcrumbs with the remaining oil and scatter over the sauce. Bake in a preheated oven, 190°C (375°F), Gas Mark 5, for 45 minutes or until golden.

MUSHROOM, COURGETTE & MASCARPONE Lasagne

1 Put the dried mushrooms in a bowl, cover with boiling water and leave to soak. Bring a large saucepan of water to the boil with 1 tablespoon of the oil. Add the pasta sheets, one at a time, and cook for about 4 minutes until just tender. Drain.

2 Meanwhile, mix together the mascarpone, garlic, dill or tarragon in a small bowl and season to taste with salt and pepper. Melt half the butter in a frying pan, add the breadcrumbs and fry gently for 2 minutes. Drain on kitchen paper.

3 Melt the remaining butter in the pan with the remaining oil. Add the fresh mushrooms and courgettes and fry for about 6 minutes until golden. Drain the dried mushrooms, add to the pan and fry for 1 minute.

4 Lay four pieces of lasagne, spaced slightly apart, in a shallow ovenproof dish. Spoon over a third of the vegetables, then a spoonful of the mascarpone mixture. Add another piece of lasagne to each stack and spoon over more vegetables and mascarpone. Finally, add the remaining lasagne, vegetables and mascarpone.

5 Scatter with the fried breadcrumbs and bake in a preheated oven, 200°C (400°F), Gas Mark 6, for 6–8 minutes until heated through.

25 g (1 oz) dried porcini mushrooms
3 tablespoons olive oil
125 g (4 oz) fresh lasagne sheets, halved
250 g (8 oz) mascarpone cheese
2 garlic cloves, crushed
3 tablespoons chopped dill or tarragon
25 g (1 oz) butter
40 g (1½ oz) fresh breadcrumbs
500 g (1 lb) cup mushrooms, sliced
2 courgettes, sliced
salt and pepper

Serves **4**
Prep time **15 minutes, plus soaking**
Cooking time **20 minutes**

VEGGIE CARBONARA

400 g (13 oz) dried penne
2 tablespoons olive oil
2 garlic cloves, finely chopped
3 courgettes, thinly sliced
6 spring onions, cut into 1 cm (¼ inch) lengths
4 egg yolks
100 ml (3¼ fl oz) crème fraîche
75 g (3 oz) Parmesan-style cheese, grated, plus extra to serve
salt and pepper

Serves 4
Prep time 5 minutes
Cooking time 10-12 minutes

1 Cook the pasta in a large saucepan of lightly salted boiling water according to the pack instructions until just tender.

2 Meanwhile, heat the oil in a heavy-based frying pan over a medium-high heat, add the garlic, courgettes and spring onions and cook, stirring, for 4–5 minutes or until the courgettes are tender. Remove the pan from the heat and set aside.

3 Put the egg yolks in a bowl and season with salt and a generous grinding of pepper. Mix together with a fork.

4 Just before the pasta is ready, return the pan with the courgette mixture to the heat. Stir in the crème fraîche and bring to the boil.

5 Drain the pasta well, return to the pan and immediately stir in the egg mixture, cheese and the creamy courgette mixture. Stir vigorously and serve immediately with a scattering of extra grated cheese.

Haloumi & ROCKET CARBONARA

1 Cook the pasta in a saucepan of lightly salted boiling water for about 10 minutes or according to the pack instructions until just tender.

2 Meanwhile, beat together the egg yolk, egg, cream, garlic and a little salt and pepper in a small bowl. Heat the oil in a frying pan and fry the haloumi for 2–3 minutes, stirring occasionally until golden.

3 Drain the pasta and return to the saucepan. Add the haloumi and the egg mixture and stir together, adding the rocket once the pasta is coated in the sauce. Keep stirring the ingredients together until the rocket has wilted slightly and the eggs have thickened in the heat of the pasta. Scatter with parsley and serve immediately.

100 g (3½ oz) dried spaghetti or linguine
1 egg yolk
1 egg
5 tablespoons single cream
1 garlic clove, crushed
2 teaspoons olive oil
75 g (3 oz) haloumi cheese, cut into small dice
25 g (1 oz) rocket leaves
salt and pepper
chopped parsley, to garnish

Serves 1
Prep time 5 minutes
Cooking time 12–15 minutes

AUBERGINE CANNELLONI

- 4 sheets of fresh or dried lasagne, each about 18 x 15 cm (7 x 6 inches)
- 2 aubergines, thinly sliced
- 4 tablespoons olive oil
- 1 teaspoon finely chopped thyme
- 250 g (8 oz) ricotta cheese
- 25 g (1 oz) basil leaves, torn into pieces
- 2 garlic cloves, crushed
- 1 quantity Tomato Sauce (see page 247)
- 100 g (3½ oz) fontina or Gruyère cheese, grated
- salt and pepper

Serves 4
Prep time **30 minutes**
Cooking time **50 minutes**

1 Bring a saucepan of salted water to the boil. Add the lasagne sheets, return to the boil and cook, allowing 2 minutes for fresh and 8–10 minutes for dried. Drain the sheets and immerse in cold water.

2 Place the aubergines in a single layer on a foil-lined grill rack. (You may need to do this in two batches.) Mix the olive oil, thyme and salt and pepper and brush over the aubergines. Grill until lightly browned, turning once.

3 Beat the ricotta with the basil, garlic and a little salt and pepper. Thoroughly drain the pasta sheets and lay them on the work surface. Cut each in half. Spread the ricotta mixture over the sheets, right to the edges. Arrange the aubergine slices on top. Roll up each piece.

4 Spread two-thirds of the tomato sauce in a shallow ovenproof dish and arrange the cannelloni on top. Spoon over the remaining tomato sauce and sprinkle with the cheese. Bake in a preheated oven, 190°C (375°F), Gas Mark 5, for 20 minutes or until the cheese is golden.

MUSHROOM TAGLIATELLE *with Gremolata*

15 g (½ oz) dried porcini mushrooms
50 g (2 oz) butter
4 tablespoons olive oil
1 small onion, finely chopped
200 g (7 oz) chestnut or button mushrooms, thinly sliced
4 tablespoons chopped herbs, such as parsley, tarragon, fennel or basil
finely grated rind of 1 lemon
2 garlic cloves, finely chopped
500 g (1 lb) fresh tagliatelle
salt and pepper

Serves **4**
Prep time **15 minutes, plus soaking**
Cooking time **10 minutes**

1 Put the porcini mushrooms in a bowl, cover with boiling water and leave to soak for 15 minutes.

2 Melt the butter with 1 tablespoon of the oil in a frying pan, add the onion and fry for 4 minutes until softened. Drain the soaked mushrooms. Thinly slice the porcini mushrooms and add them to the pan with the chestnut or button mushrooms and a quarter of the herbs. Fry gently for 5 minutes.

3 Meanwhile, cook the pasta in a large saucepan of lightly salted boiling water for about 3 minutes until just tender.

4 Make the gremolata. Mix the remaining herbs with the lemon rind, garlic and plenty of black pepper.

5 Drain the pasta and return to the saucepan. Add the mushroom mixture and toss the ingredients with the remaining oil. Serve with the gremolata.

COURGETTE & CREAMY TOMATO PENNE

400 g (13 oz) dried penne
1 tablespoon olive oil
1 onion, chopped
1 garlic clove, finely chopped
3 courgettes, chopped
1 red pepper, cored, deseeded and chopped
200 g (7 oz) mascarpone cheese
200 ml (7 fl oz) passata (sieved tomatoes)
salt and pepper
2 tablespoons chopped basil, plus extra to garnish

Serves **4**
Prep time **10 minutes**
Cooking time **15 minutes**

1 Cook the pasta in a large saucepan of lightly salted boiling water according to the pack instructions until just tender.

2 Meanwhile, heat the oil in a frying pan, add the onion and garlic and cook over a medium heat for 3 minutes until softened. Stir in the courgettes and red pepper and cook for 5 minutes until the courgettes have softened.

3 Stir the mascarpone into the pan until melted, then add the passata and simmer for 2–3 minutes. Season to taste with salt and pepper and stir in the basil.

4 Drain the pasta and return to the pan. Stir the sauce into the cooked pasta and toss well. Serve immediately with the basil scattered over.

TAGLIATELLE *with Blue Cheese Butter*

40 g (½ oz) Stilton or other creamy blue cheese
25 g (1 oz) butter, softened
pinch of grated nutmeg
75 g (3 oz) dried tagliatelle
150 g (5 oz) broccoli, cut into bite-sized pieces
salt and pepper

Serves 1
Prep time 5 minutes
Cooking time 10 minutes

1 Mash the cheese in a bowl with a fork to break it up. Add the butter, nutmeg and a little pepper and beat well to mix.

2 Cook the pasta in a large saucepan of lightly salted boiling water for 6–7 minutes until softened but not quite cooked through to the centre. Add the broccoli stalks and cook for 2 minutes, then add the tips and cook for a further 1 minute until the pasta and broccoli are tender.

3 Drain the pasta and broccoli and return to the pan. Dot half the cheese butter into the pan so it melts over the hot pasta. Dot the remaining butter into the pasta and serve immediately.

CREAMY MUSHROOM & TARRAGON RIGATONI

- 50 g (2 oz) butter
- 1 tablespoon vegetable oil
- 1 large leek, trimmed and thinly sliced
- 1 garlic clove, chopped
- 150 g (5 oz) mushrooms, sliced
- 1 teaspoon dried tarragon
- 100 ml (3½ fl oz) dry white wine or Vegetable Stock (see page 246)
- 250 ml (8 fl oz) single cream
- 400 g (13 oz) dried rigatoni or tortiglioni pasta
- salt and pepper
- 4 teaspoons grated Parmesan-style cheese, to serve

Serves **4**
Prep time **5 minutes**
Cooking time **15 minutes**

1 Heat the butter and oil in a large nonstick frying pan until the butter is frothing. Add the leek and garlic and cook for 2–3 minutes until beginning to soften. Add the mushrooms and tarragon and cook for a further 4–5 minutes until soft and golden.

2 Pour the white wine or vegetable stock and cream into the mushrooms, then season generously with salt and pepper. Simmer gently for 6–7 minutes.

3 Meanwhile, cook the pasta in a large saucepan of lightly salted boiling water for 11 minutes or according to the pack instructions until just tender.

4 Drain the pasta and stir into the sauce. Serve immediately, sprinkled with grated cheese.

RIBBON PASTA
WITH AUBERGINES & PINE NUTS

8 tablespoons olive oil
2 aubergines, diced
2 red onions, sliced
75 g (3 oz) pine nuts
3 garlic cloves, crushed
5 tablespoons sun-dried tomato paste
150 ml (¼ pint) Vegetable Stock (see page 246)
300 g (10 oz) fresh ribbon pasta
100 g (3½ oz) pitted black olives
salt and pepper
3 tablespoons roughly chopped flat leaf parsley, to garnish

1 Heat the oil in a large frying pan, add the aubergines and onions and fry for 8–10 minutes until golden and tender. Add the pine nuts and garlic and fry for 2 minutes. Stir in the sun-dried tomato paste and stock and cook for 2 minutes.

2 Meanwhile, cook the pasta in a large saucepan of lightly salted boiling water for about 2 minutes or until just tender.

3 Drain the pasta and return to the pan. Add the sauce and olives, season to taste with salt and pepper and toss together over a medium heat for 1 minute until combined. Scatter with parsley and serve immediately.

Serves **4**
Prep time **5 minutes**
Cooking time **15 minutes**

GOATS' CHEESE LINGUINE

WITH GARLIC & HERB BUTTER

1 Thickly slice the goats' cheese and arrange on a lightly oiled, foil-lined grill rack. Grill under a preheated hot grill for about 2 minutes until golden. Keep warm.

2 Using a zester, pare rind strips from the lemon, then squeeze the juice.

3 Heat the butter and oil in a frying pan, add the shallots and garlic and fry gently for 3 minutes. Stir in the herbs, capers and lemon juice, and season to taste with salt and pepper.

4 Meanwhile, cook the pasta in a saucepan of lightly salted boiling water for about 2 minutes or until just tender. Drain lightly and return to the saucepan. Add the goats' cheese and herb butter sauce and toss the ingredients together gently. Serve scattered with strips of lemon rind.

300 g (10 oz) firm goats' cheese
1 lemon
2 tablespoons olive oil, plus extra for oiling
75 g (3 oz) butter
3 shallots, finely chopped
2 garlic cloves, crushed
25 g (1 oz) mixed chopped herbs, such as tarragon, chervil, parsley and dill
3 tablespoons capers, drained
300 g (10 oz) fresh linguine
salt and pepper

Serves **4**
Prep time **5 minutes**
Cooking time **7 minutes**

PASTA WITH FENNEL & ROCKET

- 1 tablespoon olive oil
- 1 fennel bulb, trimmed and thinly sliced
- 1 garlic clove, chopped
- 100 ml (3½ fl oz) dry white wine
- 4 tablespoons crème fraîche
- grated rind and juice of 1 small lemon
- 50 g (2 oz) rocket leaves
- 250 g (8 oz) fresh tagliatelle or pappardelle
- salt and pepper
- grated Parmesan-style cheese, to serve

Serves 2
Prep time **10 minutes**
Cooking time **15 minutes**

1 Heat the oil in a frying pan, add the fennel and garlic and cook gently for about 10 minutes until the fennel is soft and golden.

2 Add the wine to the pan and cook until reduced by half. Stir in the crème fraîche, lemon rind and juice and rocket and cook, stirring, until the rocket has wilted. Season to taste with salt and pepper.

3 Meanwhile, cook the pasta in a large saucepan of lightly salted boiling water for 3–4 minutes or according to the pack instructions until just tender. Drain and return to the pan.

4 Stir the sauce into the cooked pasta and toss well. Season with freshly ground black pepper and serve immediately with the cheese.

MACARONI CHEESE WITH SPINACH

300 g (10 oz) dried macaroni
50 g (2 oz) butter
50 g (2 oz) plain flour
750 ml (¼ pints) milk
150 g (5 oz) Taleggio or fontina cheese, chopped
2 teaspoons wholegrain mustard
1 teaspoon Dijon mustard
350 g (11½ oz) baby spinach leaves
8 cherry tomatoes, halved
50 g (2 oz) fresh white breadcrumbs
25 g (1 oz) Cheddar cheese, finely grated
salt and pepper

Serves **4**
Prep time **10 minutes**
Cooking time **30 minutes**

1 Cook the macaroni in a large saucepan of lightly salted boiling water for 8–10 minutes or according to the pack instructions until just tender.

2 Meanwhile, place the butter, flour and milk in a saucepan and whisk constantly over a medium heat until the sauce boils and thickens. Simmer for 2–3 minutes until you have a smooth glossy sauce, then reduce the heat to low and stir in the Taleggio or fontina and mustards. Season to taste with salt and pepper and cook gently until the cheese has melted.

3 Add the spinach to the pasta pan and cook for a further 1 minute until wilted. Drain well and place in a 1.5 litre (2½ pint) ovenproof dish.

4 Pour the sauce over the macaroni and spinach, scatter over the tomatoes and then sprinkle with the breadcrumbs and Cheddar. Bake in a preheated oven, 200°C (400°F), Gas Mark 6, for 20 minutes until golden and bubbling.

MUSHROOM, EGG & CRESS ALL-DAY PIZZA

1 Preheat oven to 250°C (480°F), Gas Mark 8. Mix the warm milk and water in a jug with the fresh yeast, if using, and sugar. Leave to stand for about 15 minutes until frothy.

2 Put the flour, yeast, salt and 2 tablespoons of the oil in a bowl. (If using dried yeast omit the first step and combine all the dough ingredients in a bowl.) Mix to a soft dough with a round-bladed knife. Turn out on to a floured surface and knead for 10 minutes until the dough is smooth and elastic. Put in a lightly oiled bowl, cover with clingfilm and leave to rise in a warm place for about 45 minutes until risen to twice the size.

3 Mix the remaining oil with the garlic and a little salt and pepper. Turn the dough out on to a floured surface and cut in half. Roll out each piece until roughly 23 cm (9 inches) in diameter and transfer to baking sheets.

4 Scatter the mushrooms over one side of each pizza. Brush the garlic oil over the pizzas and mushroom slices and leave to stand for 10 minutes.

5 Carefully break 2 eggs on to each pizza, season with pepper and bake for 12 minutes until both pizza base and eggs are cooked through. Serve scattered with cress.

125 ml (4 fl oz) mixed milk and water, lukewarm
15 g (½ oz) fresh yeast or 1 teaspoon fast-action dried yeast
½ teaspoon caster sugar
175 g (6 oz) strong white bread flour, plus extra for dusting
½ teaspoon salt
3 tablespoons olive oil, plus extra for greasing
1 garlic clove, crushed
2 large portobello mushrooms, sliced
4 eggs
1 punnet of cress
salt and pepper

Serves 2
Prep time **25 minutes, plus standing and proving**
Cooking time **12 minutes**

SWISS CHEESE MELTS

1 large French stick
200 g (7 oz) Swiss cheese, such as Emmental or Gruyère, grated
1 tablespoon wholegrain mustard
2 tablespoons mayonnaise
2 tomatoes, deseeded and chopped
pinch of black pepper
1 round lettuce, to serve (optional)

Serves **4**
Prep time **10 minutes**
Cooking time **3-4 minutes**

1 Cut the French stick in half, then slice each half horizontally to form four long pieces. Place the grated cheese in a bowl with the remaining ingredients and mix well to combine.

2 Spoon the topping over the cut side of each piece of bread and place on a baking sheet. Cook under a preheated hot grill for 3–4 minutes until golden and bubbling. Serve hot with lettuce leaves, if liked.

STUDENT TIP

Give dirty pans and plates a quick rinse when you've finished using them. If you can't face washing up after dinner, the water will loosen the worst of the food and you won't have to spend ages scrubbing off dried chunks the next morning. Better still, soak them in soapy water.

SPICY MEXICAN WRAPS

1 Heat the oil in a saucepan, add the onion and fry for 5 minutes until softened. Stir in the garlic and spices and cook for a further 1 minute.

2 Add the beans, tomatoes, ketchup and a little salt and bring to the boil. Reduce the heat to its lowest setting and cook gently for 15–20 minutes until thick and pulpy.

3 Meanwhile, halve the avocado and discard the stone. Peel away the skin and thinly slice the flesh.

4 Heat a dry frying pan and warm the tortillas through briefly. Spread each wrap with a layer of bean mixture, scatter with cheese and avocado slices and dot with soured cream. Roll up to enclose the filling and serve.

2 tablespoons vegetable oil
1 onion, chopped
1 garlic clove, finely chopped
½ teaspoon ground coriander
½ teaspoon ground cumin
1 teaspoon mild chilli powder
400 g (13 oz) can red kidney beans, rinsed and drained
400 g (13 oz) can chopped tomatoes
2 tablespoons tomato ketchup
1 avocado
4 seeded tortilla wraps
75 g (3 oz) mature Cheddar cheese, grated
4 tablespoons soured cream
salt

Serves **4**
Prep time **15 minutes**
Cooking time **25–30 minutes**

AFFORDABILITY 1

TORTILLAS *with minted chilli* & AUBERGINE YOGURT

4 tablespoons olive oil
1 aubergine, thinly sliced
small handful of mint, chopped
small handful of parsley, chopped
2 tablespoons chopped chives
1 green chilli, deseeded and thinly sliced
200 ml (7 fl oz) Greek yogurt
2 tablespoons mayonnaise
2 large tortillas
7 cm (3 inch) length of cucumber, thinly sliced
salt and pepper
paprika, to garnish

Serves **2**
Prep time **10 minutes, plus cooling**
Cooking time **10 minutes**

1 Heat the oil in a frying pan, add the aubergine and fry for about 10 minutes until golden. Drain and leave to cool.

2 Mix the herbs with the chilli, yogurt and mayonnaise in a bowl and season to taste with salt and pepper.

3 Arrange the fried aubergine slices over the tortillas and spread with the Greek yogurt mixture. Arrange the cucumber slices on top. Roll up each tortilla, sprinkle with paprika and serve.

Camembert WRAPS WITH HOT PEPPER SALSA

2 tablespoons vegetable oil
1 red onion, chopped
2 celery sticks, chopped
2 red peppers, cored, deseeded and chopped
1 yellow pepper, cored, deseeded and chopped
4 tablespoons chopped fresh coriander
2 teaspoons white wine vinegar
2 teaspoons clear honey
250 g (8 oz) round Camembert cheese
4 tortilla wraps
50 g (2 oz) pea shoots or mixed salad leaves
salt and pepper

Serves **4**
Prep time **20 minutes**
Cooking time **25 minutes**

1 Heat the oil in a frying pan, add the onion, celery and peppers and fry gently for 15 minutes or until softened and lightly browned. Stir in the coriander, vinegar and honey and season to taste.

2 Place the camembert on a board and slice horizontally into 4 thin rounds. Place a round on top of each tortilla and position two of them on separate baking sheets. Cook in a preheated oven, 200°C (400°F), Gas Mark 6, for 3–4 minutes until the cheese has softened. Remove from the oven and cook the remaining two in the same way.

3 Spread the softened cheese towards the edges of the tortillas with the back of a spoon. Spread the pepper mixture on top and scatter with the leaves. Roll up the tortillas and serve.

2 tablespoons vegetable oil
1 red onion, chopped
3 garlic cloves, crushed
150 g (5 oz) red rice, rinsed
500 ml (17 fl oz) Vegetable Stock (see page 246)
1 cinnamon stick (optional)
8 cardamom pods, crushed to expose the seeds
1 peach or nectarine, halved, stoned and diced
3 tablespoons chopped mint
50 g (2 oz) chopped nuts, such as almonds, hazelnuts or walnuts

Kale crisps
100 g (3½ oz) kale
1 tablespoon olive oil
salt and pepper

Serves **2**
Prep time **20 minutes**
Cooking time **50 minutes**

1 Heat the vegetable oil in a saucepan, add the onion and gently fry for 5 minutes. Add the garlic and rice and cook for a further 2 minutes. Pour in the stock and bring to a gentle simmer. Add the cinnamon, if using, and cardamom, cover with a lid and cook very gently for 40 minutes until the rice is tender and the stock is absorbed.

2 Meanwhile, thoroughly wash and dry the kale (a salad spinner is ideal but you can also pat it dry between layers of kitchen paper). Tear into pieces if the kale hasn't already been prepared, discarding any thick stalks. Drizzle the oil over the kale with a little salt and pepper. Mix well.

3 Tip out on to a baking sheet and bake in a preheated oven, 180°C (350°F), Gas Mark 4, for 10 minutes until crisp. Take care not to overcook the kale or it'll turn bitter.

4 Stir the peach or nectarine, mint and nuts into the rice. Season to taste and transfer to warmed serving plates. Scatter the kale on top and serve.

Creamy Mushroom & Chive Risotto

50 g (2 oz) butter
1 onion, finely chopped
2 garlic cloves, finely chopped
300 g (10 oz) mushrooms, preferably brown-cap, chopped
350 g (11½ oz) risotto rice
125 ml (4 fl oz) dry white wine (optional)
1.2 litres (2 pints) hot Vegetable Stock (see page 246) (add an extra 125 ml/4 fl oz if not using wine)
3 tablespoons crème fraîche
2 tablespoons chopped chives
salt and pepper
grated Parmesan-style cheese, to serve (optional)

Serves **4**
Prep time **10 minutes**
Cooking time **30 minutes**

1 Melt the butter in a pan, add the onion and garlic and cook over a medium heat for 4–5 minutes. Add the mushrooms and cook for 2–3 minutes, stirring occasionally. Add the risotto rice and cook, stirring, for 1 minute. Pour in the white wine, if using, and simmer rapidly for about 1 minute until the wine is absorbed.

2 Add a small ladleful of hot stock and cook, stirring frequently, until almost absorbed. Add a little more stock and continue cooking, stirring frequently, until almost absorbed. Continue in the same way until all the stock is used and the rice is creamy but still retaining a little bite. This will take about 20 minutes.

3 Stir the crème fraîche and chives into the risotto and season well. Remove from the heat, cover with a lid and leave to stand for 2 minutes. Serve sprinkled with grated cheese.

AFFORDABILITY
1

EASY PEA RISOTTO

25 g (1 oz) butter
1 onion, finely chopped
1 garlic clove, crushed
150 g (5 oz) risotto rice
500 ml (17 fl oz) hot Vegetable Stock (see page 246)
150 g (5 oz) frozen peas
4 tablespoons chopped chives
2 tablespoons chopped dill
salt and pepper
grated Parmesan-style cheese, to serve

Serves 2
Prep time **10 minutes**
Cooking time **40 minutes**

1 Melt the butter in a flameproof casserole, add the onion and fry for 5 minutes until softened. Add the garlic and rice and cook, stirring, for 1 minute until coated in the butter. Stir in the stock and bring to the boil. (If you don't have a flameproof casserole, fry the ingredients in a saucepan and transfer to a baking dish.)

2 Cover with a lid or foil and bake in a preheated oven, 180°C (350°F), Gas Mark 4, for 15 minutes. Stir in the peas, chives and dill and return to the oven for a further 10 minutes until the peas are cooked through. If the risotto has dried out, stir in a splash of water.

3 Season to taste and serve sprinkled with plenty of grated cheese.

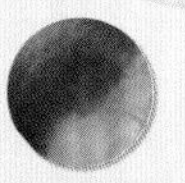

STUDENT TIP

If you're used to the luxury of branded food it might be a shock to the system to fill up your basket with own-brand equivalents. However, these days a lot of own-label foods are indistinguishable from their big-brand counterparts and your weekly shop will work out a lot cheaper.

BEETROOT RISOTTO

with Horseradish & MIXED LEAVES

IF YOU CAN FIND FRESH HORSERADISH, USE IT IN PLACE OF THE BOTTLED VARIETY. THE FLAVOUR IS FAR SUPERIOR, BUT BEWARE OF ITS HEAT INTENSITY WHICH CAN BE ANYTHING FROM HARMLESSLY MILD TO HOT AND FIERY, DEPENDING ON ITS FRESHNESS.

4 tablespoons olive oil
1 large red onion, chopped
3 garlic cloves, crushed
400 g (14 oz) risotto rice
1.3 litres (2¾ pints) hot Vegetable Stock (see page 246)
425 g (14 oz) cooked beetroot, finely diced
4 tablespoons roughly chopped dill
1–2 tablespoons freshly grated horseradish or 1 tablespoon hot horseradish from a jar
50 g (2 oz) salted macadamia nuts or almonds
salt and pepper
mixed salad leaves, to serve

Serves 4
Prep time **5 minutes**
Cooking time **25 minutes**

1 Heat the oil in a large, heavy-based saucepan, add the onion and garlic and fry gently for 3 minutes. Add the rice and cook, stirring, for 1 minute.

2 Add 2 ladlefuls of the stock and cook, stirring frequently, until almost absorbed. Add a little more stock and continue cooking, stirring frequently, until almost absorbed. Continue in the same way until all the stock is used and the rice is creamy but still retaining a little bite. This will take about 20 minutes.

3 Stir in the beetroot, dill, horseradish and nuts, season to taste and heat through gently for 1 minute. Serve scattered with mixed salad leaves.

Lemon & Herb RISOTTO

1 Heat the oil in a heavy-based saucepan, add the shallots, garlic, celery, courgette and carrot and fry over a low heat for 4 minutes or until the vegetables have softened. Add the rice, increase the heat and cook, stirring, for 2–3 minutes.

2 Add a ladleful of hot stock, half the herbs and season well. Cook, stirring frequently, until the stock is almost absorbed. Reduce the heat to medium-low, add a little more stock and continue cooking, stirring constantly, until almost absorbed. Continue in the same way until all the stock is used and the rice is cooked through but still retaining a little bite. This will take about 20 minutes.

3 Remove from the heat and gently stir in the remaining herbs, butter, lemon rind and cheese. Cover with a lid and leave to stand for 2–3 minutes, during which time it will become creamy and oozy. Serve immediately, sprinkled with freshly ground black pepper.

1 tablespoon olive oil
3 shallots, finely chopped
2 garlic cloves, finely chopped
½ head of celery, finely chopped
1 courgette, finely diced
1 carrot, peeled and finely diced
300 g (10 oz) risotto rice
1.2 litres (2 pints) hot Vegetable Stock (see page 246)
large handful of fresh mixed herbs, such as tarragon, parsley, chives and dill
100 g (3½ oz) butter
1 tablespoon finely grated lemon rind
100 g (3½ oz) Parmesan-style cheese, grated
salt and pepper

Serves **4**
Prep time **10 minutes**
Cooking time **30 minutes**

COOKING TIP

If you use a lot of fresh herbs in cooking try growing your own. You don't need outside space – a windowsill will do – and hardy herbs such as rosemary and thyme can be used to liven up all sorts of dishes.

SAGE & TOMATO PILAF V

1 Cut each tomato into eight and thickly slice the pepper quarters. Place in a roasting tin with the onion, then drizzle with the oil and season well. Tear some of the sage into pieces and sprinkle over the vegetables. Roast in a preheated oven, 200°C (400°F), Gas Mark 6, for 40–45 minutes until softened.

2 Meanwhile, cook the rice in a saucepan of boiling water for 15 minutes or until tender. Drain well.

3 Mix the rice into the cooked tomatoes and peppers, then sprinkle with the remaining sage leaves. Serve with warm bread.

500 g (1 lb) plum tomatoes
1 red pepper, cored, deseeded and quartered
1 onion, roughly chopped
2 tablespoons olive oil
1 small bunch of sage
200 g (7 oz) easy-cook long grain white and wild rice mixed
salt and pepper
warm ciabatta or herb bread, to serve

Serves **4**
Prep time **15 minutes**
Cooking time **40–45 minutes**

CARROT & FETA
Potato Cakes

1 Cook the carrots and potatoes in a large saucepan of lightly salted boiling water for about 12 minutes until tender. Drain well and mash together until crushed but not completely smooth. Leave to cool, uncovered, for at least 10 minutes.

2 While the potatoes and carrots are cooling, add the beaten egg, feta, cumin, parsley, spring onions and a pinch each of salt and pepper to the pan and mix well to combine. Use flour-dusted hands to shape the mixture into four patties.

3 Heat the oil in a large nonstick frying pan and shallow-fry the patties gently for about 3 minutes on each side until crisp and golden. Drain on kitchen paper and serve with fried or poached eggs, if liked.

150 g (5 oz) or 1 large carrot, peeled and diced
350 g (11½ oz) potatoes, peeled and diced
1 small egg, lightly beaten
75 g (3 oz) feta cheese, crumbled
1 teaspoon ground cumin
1 tablespoon chopped parsley (optional)
2 spring onions, chopped
flour, for dusting
3–4 tablespoons vegetable oil
salt and pepper
2 poached or fried eggs, to serve (optional)

Serves **2**
Prep time **15 minutes, plus cooling**
Cooking time **20 minutes**

WARM MUSHROOMS WITH POTATO ROSTI

1 Cook the potatoes whole in a large saucepan of lightly salted boiling water for 8–10 minutes. Drain and set aside to cool slightly. Coarsely grate the potatoes and mix in a bowl with the sliced onion, 2 tablespoons oil and plenty of salt and pepper.

2 Heat the remaining oil in a large nonstick frying pan and add the rosti mixture, pushing down to flatten it so that it covers the base of the pan. Cook for 7–8 minutes, then slide on to an oiled plate or board. Flip the rosti back into the pan to cook the other side for 7–8 minutes until crisp and golden.

3 Meanwhile, melt the butter in a frying pan and cook the garlic and mushrooms gently for 6–7 minutes, until golden. Season to taste with salt and pepper, then stir in the chopped parsley, if using. Cut the rosti into wedges, then arrange on serving plates, scatter over the watercress and spoon over the warm mushrooms with their juices. Serve immediately.

3 potatoes, scrubbed but unpeeled, about 625 g (1¼ lb) total weight
½ onion, very thinly sliced
4 tablespoons vegetable oil
50 g (2 oz) butter
1 garlic clove, chopped
250 g (8 oz) button mushrooms, thinly sliced
2 tablespoons finely chopped parsley (optional)
salt and pepper
1 large bunch of watercress, to serve

Serves **4**
Prep time **15 minutes**
Cooking time **20–25 minutes**

Chimichurri CHIPS & BEANS

1 Scrub or peel the sweet potatoes and cut into chunky chips. Scatter in a roasting tin with the red onions, drizzle with 1 tablespoon of the oil and mix together. Bake in a preheated oven, 200°C (400°F), Gas Mark 6, for 25 minutes until the potatoes are golden and just tender. Stir once or twice during cooking so the vegetables brown evenly.

2 Blend the cornflour with 2 tablespoons cold water in a small bowl. Add the lime rind and half the juice, the sugar, soy sauce and butter beans. Stir well.

3 Tip the mixture over the potatoes, mix well and return to the oven for 10 minutes, stirring the ingredients after 5 minutes so the juices thicken evenly.

4 Mix the remaining oil with the chilli flakes, parsley, coriander, spring onions and remaining lime juice. Spoon the vegetables and beans on to warmed serving plates and drizzle with the sauce.

450 g (14¾ oz) sweet potatoes
2 red onions, cut into wedges
3 tablespoons vegetable oil
1 teaspoon cornflour
finely grated rind and juice of 1 lime
2 teaspoons light muscovado or caster sugar
2 tablespoons soy sauce
400 g (14 oz) can butter beans, rinsed and drained
¼ teaspoon dried chilli flakes
3 tablespoons chopped parsley
3 tablespoons chopped fresh coriander
2 spring onions, finely chopped

Serves **2**
Prep time **15 minutes**
Cooking time **35 minutes**

Jamaican COCONUT CURRY

1 Heat the oil in a large frying pan or saucepan, add the ginger, chilli, ground spices and onions and cook very gently for about 5 minutes, stirring occasionally, until the onions have softened. Add the garlic and fry for a further 1 minute.

2 Add the potatoes to the pan with the stock and coconut cream. Bring to a gentle simmer, cover with a lid and cook gently for 20–25 minutes until the potatoes are tender.

3 Add the tomatoes, courgettes and peas and cook for 15 minutes until all the vegetables are tender and the juices are beginning to thicken. Season to taste and serve with lemon or lime wedges for squeezing over the curry.

4 tablespoons vegetable oil
50 g (2 oz) fresh root ginger, peeled and grated
1 red chilli, deseeded and finely chopped
2 teaspoons ground cumin
2 teaspoons ground coriander
1 teaspoon turmeric
2 onions, roughly chopped
4 garlic cloves, crushed
750 g (1½ lb) Charlotte or salad potatoes, cut into 1.5 cm (¾ inch) chunks
300 ml (½ pint) Vegetable Stock (see page 246)
160 ml (5½ fl oz) can coconut cream
2 tomatoes, skinned and chopped
2 small courgettes, thinly sliced
100 g (3½ oz) peas
salt and pepper
lemon or lime wedges, to serve

Serves **3–4**
Prep time **25 minutes**
Cooking time **45–50 minutes**

VEGETABLE NOODLES in Spiced Coconut Milk

A SINGLE THAI CHILLI GIVES THIS DISH A REALLY FIERY KICK. SUBSTITUTE A MILD CHILLI IF YOU ARE FEELING CAUTIOUS!

1 Place the noodles in a bowl, cover with boiling water and leave to stand while preparing the vegetables.

2 Heat the oil in a large saucepan, add the onion, chilli, garlic, ginger, coriander, turmeric and lemon grass and fry gently for 5 minutes.

3 Drain the noodles. Add the coconut milk and stock to the pan and bring just to the boil. Reduce the heat and stir in the spring greens or cabbage, beans, mushrooms and drained noodles. Cover with a lid and simmer for 5 minutes. Stir in the peanuts and season to taste with salt and pepper. Serve immediately.

125 g (4 oz) dried medium egg noodles
2 tablespoons vegetable oil
1 onion, chopped
1 red chilli, deseeded and sliced
3 garlic cloves, sliced
5 cm (2 inch) piece of fresh root ginger, peeled and grated
2 teaspoons ground coriander
½ teaspoon turmeric
1 lemon grass stalk, finely sliced
400 ml (14 fl oz) can coconut milk
300 ml (½ pint) Vegetable Stock (see page 246)
125 g (4 oz) spring greens or cabbage, finely shredded
275 g (9 oz) runner beans or green beans, trimmed and sliced diagonally
150 g (5 oz) shiitake mushrooms, sliced
75 g (3 oz) raw, unsalted peanuts
salt and pepper

Serves **4**
Prep time **15 minutes**
Cooking time **15 minutes**

EAT YOURSELF *Healthy*

Students get a rap for their unhealthy eating habits and the combination of budget, time and skill constraints means this is often justified. If you've been fortunate enough to be treated like a guest in a restaurant for most of your mealtimes while living at home, there has probably been little incentive to dice and slice your way to your own dinner. However, eating a balanced, healthy diet will not only sharpen your brain cells and keep you alert during the dullest lecture, it will also boost your body's immune system against coughs, colds and viruses. Infectious bugs rampage through student households like wildfire so if you can give yourself a head start on warding them off, so much the better.

THE HEALTHY VEGGIE

As a vegetarian you have a bit more planning and preparation to do than your carnivore classmates. Protein and iron are the two elements that a veggie student diet may well be lacking so it's important to make sure you include these by eating plenty of dairy produce, eggs and grains (for protein) and nuts, green vegetables and dried fruit (for iron).

HIGH FIVE

Getting your five a day should be second nature to a vegetarian, as you will be substituting fish and meat for larger portions and a greater range of fresh fruit and vegetables. This is where market shopping comes into its own – supermarket produce can be surprisingly expensive for non-staples, so it makes sense to shop around and make use of local markets and vegetable stalls.

CARB-LOADING

Carbohydrates are energy foods – and that doesn't mean sports drinks, lattes and chocolate bars. We're talking about slow-release energy that will keep you going throughout the day, rather than giving you a quick burst at breakfast time and leaving you with a sugar crash by the time you get into college. Bread, rice and pasta are all excellent sources of cheap and nutritious carbohydrates but you need to swap white for wholemeal varieties in order to get the most benefit and maximize your energy levels.

KEEP FIT

Lethargy is a common curse of the student lifestyle and it's easy to fall into the habit of sleeping, slouching and sitting around. If you live close to campus you can shave pounds off your love handles and your weekly budget by ditching the bus and walking or cycling to lectures. Alternatively, swap one evening a week in the student union for an evening in the gym or at sports practice.

HOT & SPICY VEGETABLE NOODLES

2 tablespoons vegetable oil
2 garlic cloves, thinly sliced
1 mild red chilli, deseeded and finely chopped
1 bunch of spring onions, sliced
600 ml (1 pint) Vegetable Stock (see page 246)
1 tablespoon soy sauce
1 large courgette, diced
100 g (3½ oz) baby corn, halved
15 g (½ oz) piece of fresh root ginger, peeled and grated
100 g (3½ oz) rice noodles
100 g (3½ oz) spinach leaves, tough stalks removed

Serves **2**
Prep time **10 minutes**
Cooking time **20 minutes**

1 Heat the oil in a large saucepan or wok, add the garlic, chilli and spring onions and fry for 30 seconds. Stir in the stock, soy sauce, courgette, baby corn and ginger.

2 Bring to the boil, then reduce the heat to its lowest setting, cover with a lid and cook gently for 10 minutes.

3 Stir in the rice noodles and cook for several minutes or until they start to soften. Add the spinach and cook for a further 2–3 minutes, stirring to combine the ingredients. Serve in deep warmed bowls.

STUDENT TIP

It goes without saying that you should never go the supermarket on an empty stomach. Hunger can do strange things to a budget and shopping list – before you know it, you'll have a trolley full of biscuits and nothing to create a healthy meal.

BLACK BEAN SOUP *with Soba Noodles*

1 Cook the noodles in a saucepan of boiling water for about 5 minutes or until just tender.

2 Meanwhile, heat the oil in a saucepan, add the spring onions and garlic and fry gently for 1 minute.

3 Add the chilli, ginger, black bean sauce and stock and bring to the boil. Stir in the pak choi or spring greens, soy sauce, sugar and peanuts, reduce the heat and simmer gently, uncovered, for 4 minutes.

4 Drain the noodles and pile into warmed serving bowls. Ladle over the soup and serve immediately.

200 g (7 oz) dried soba noodles
2 tablespoons vegetable oil
1 bunch of spring onions, sliced
2 garlic cloves, roughly chopped
1 red chilli, deseeded and sliced
4 cm (1½ inch) piece of fresh root ginger, peeled and grated
125 ml (4 fl oz) black bean sauce or black bean stir-fry sauce
750 ml (1½ pints) Vegetable Stock (see page 246)
200 g (7 oz) pak choi or spring greens, shredded
2 teaspoons soy sauce
1 teaspoon caster sugar
50 g (2 oz) raw, unsalted peanuts

Serves **4**
Prep time **5 minutes**
Cooking time **10 minutes**

V

Rice Noodle Pancakes WITH STIR-FRIED VEGETABLES

175 g (6 oz) dried ribbon rice noodles
1 green chilli, deseeded and sliced
2.5 cm (1 inch) piece of fresh root ginger, peeled and grated
3 tablespoons chopped fresh coriander
2 teaspoons plain flour
2 teaspoons vegetable oil, plus extra for shallow-frying

Stir-fried vegetables
125 g (4 oz) broccoli
2 tablespoons vegetable oil
1 small onion, sliced
1 red pepper, cored, deseeded and sliced
1 yellow or orange pepper, cored, deseeded and sliced
125 g (4 oz) sugar snap peas, halved lengthways
6 tablespoons hoisin sauce
1 tablespoon lime juice
salt and pepper

Serves **4**
Prep time **15 minutes**
Cooking time **15 minutes**

1 Cook the noodles in a saucepan of lightly salted boiling water for 3 minutes or until tender. Drain well. Transfer to a bowl, then add the chilli, ginger, coriander, flour and the 2 teaspoons oil and mix well. Set aside.

2 Thinly slice the broccoli stalks and cut the florets into small pieces. Cook the stalks in boiling water for 30 seconds, add the florets and cook for a further 30 seconds. Drain.

3 Heat the 2 tablespoons oil in a wok or large frying pan, add the onion and stir-fry for 2 minutes. Add the peppers and stir-fry for 3 minutes until softened but still retaining texture. Stir in the cooked broccoli, sugar snap peas, hoisin sauce and lime juice, season to taste with salt and pepper and set aside.

4 Heat 1 cm (½ inch) oil in a frying pan. Place four large separate spoonfuls of the noodles (half the mixture) in the oil. Fry for about 5 minutes until crisp and lightly coloured. Drain the pancakes on kitchen paper and keep warm while cooking the remaining noodle mixture in the same way.

5 Heat the vegetables through for 1 minute in the wok or frying pan. Place two pancakes on each warmed serving plate and pile the stir-fried vegetables on top.

AFFORDABILITY
1

186 VEGAN LUNCHBOWL SALAD
187 GADO GADO SALAD
188 HEALTHY GREEN BEAN & MIDDLE EASTERN BREAD SALAD
189 MIDDLE EASTERN BREAD SALAD
190 SWEET POTATO, ROCKET & HALOUMI SALAD
191 PANZANELLA
192 WARM AUBERGINE SALAD
193 WARM PASTA SALAD WITH LEMON & BROCCOLI
194 MUSHROOM & EGG FRIED RICE
196 TABBOULEH WITH FRUIT & NUTS
197 SWEET POTATO & GARLIC MASH
198 BAKED SWEET POTATOES
199 CRISP PARSNIP CAKES
200 CORN & COURGETTE CAKES
201 CHARGRILLED POLENTA TRIANGLES
202 MUSTARD RAREBIT
204 GARLIC & BEAN PÂTÉ
205 RED CABBAGE & BEETROOT LENTILS
206 RED CABBAGE COLESLAW
207 POTATO TORTILLA
207 CHUNKY POTATO CHIPS

WARM PASTA SALAD WITH LEMON & BROCCOLI

Salads, Sides & Snacks

MUSTARD RAREBIT

BAKED SWEET POTATO

CORN & COURGETTE CAKES

VEGAN LUNCHBOWL SALAD

75 g (3 oz) quinoa, rinsed
1 teaspoon vegan vegetable bouillon powder
½ red pepper, deseeded and thinly sliced
½ small fennel bulb, thinly sliced
½ Little Gem lettuce, finely shredded
handful of basil leaves, shredded

Dressing
1 teaspoon harissa paste
3 tablespoons olive oil
2 teaspoons white or red wine vinegar
1 teaspoon caster sugar
salt

Serves **1**
Prep time **15 minutes, plus cooling**
Cooking time **15 minutes**

1 Put the quinoa in a saucepan with the bouillon powder and 200 ml (7 fl oz) boiling water, cover with a lid and cook very gently for 15 minutes until the quinoa is tender and the water absorbed. If there's still quite a lot of liquid in the pan, increase the heat, remove the lid and cook for a couple of minutes so the liquid evaporates.

2 Tip the quinoa into a bowl and stir in the red pepper and fennel. Leave to cool.

3 Beat together the dressing ingredients. Stir the lettuce, basil and dressing into the salad to serve.

Gado Gado Salad

4 eggs
1 iceberg lettuce, roughly chopped
2 carrots, peeled and cut into matchsticks
½ cucumber, peeled and cut into matchsticks
½ red pepper, cored, deseeded and cut into matchsticks

Peanut dressing
4 tablespoons crunchy peanut butter
juice of 1 lime
1 tablespoon clear honey
1 tablespoon soy sauce
½ teaspoon finely chopped red chilli

Serves **4**
Prep time **15 minutes**
Cooking time **15 minutes**

1 Put the eggs in a saucepan of cold water and bring to the boil. Cook for 10 minutes, then plunge into cold water to cool. Shell the eggs, then cut them in half lengthways. Combine all the remaining salad ingredients in a bowl or arrange on a plate, then add the egg halves.

2 Put all the dressing ingredients in a saucepan and heat gently, stirring, until combined. Drizzle the dressing over the salad and serve immediately or serve the dressing as a dipping sauce for the salad.

HEALTHY GREEN BEAN & BROCCOLI SALAD

V

200 g (7 oz) mixture of broccoli florets and fine green beans
400 g (13 oz) can borlotti or aduki beans, rinsed and drained
1 celery stick, finely chopped
½ small red onion, finely sliced
1 small ripe avocado, peeled, stoned and diced
1 tablespoon sunflower seeds

Dressing
1 tablespoon lime or lemon juice
2 tablespoons vegetable oil
1 tablespoon light soy sauce

Serves **2**
Prep time **10 minutes**
Cooking time **2-3 minutes**

1 Cook the green beans and broccoli in a saucepan of lightly salted boiling water for 2-3 minutes until just tender. Drain and cool under cold running water, then drain again.

2 Meanwhile, combine the canned beans in a bowl with the celery, onion and avocado.

3 Whisk together the dressing ingredients in a small bowl.

4 Add the green beans and broccoli to the salad and gently fold through the dressing. Spoon into a serving dish and scatter with the sunflower seeds.

MIDDLE EASTERN BREAD SALAD

2 flatbreads or flour tortillas
1 large green pepper, cored, deseeded and diced
1 Lebanese cucumber, diced
250 g (8 oz) cherry tomatoes, halved
½ red onion, finely chopped
2 tablespoons chopped mint
2 tablespoons chopped parsley
2 tablespoons chopped fresh coriander
3 tablespoons olive oil
juice of 1 lemon
salt and pepper

Serves **4–6**
Prep time **10 minutes, plus cooling**
Cooking time **2–3 minutes**

1 Cook the flatbreads under a preheated hot grill for 2–3 minutes until toasted and charred. Leave to cool, then tear into bite-sized pieces.

2 Put the green pepper, cucumber, tomatoes, onion and herbs in a bowl, add the oil, lemon juice and salt and pepper and stir well. Add the bread and stir again. Serve immediately.

SWEET POTATO, ROCKET & Haloumi Salad

THIS COMBINATION OF FIRM, SALTY CHEESE, SWEET POTATO AND A HONEYED, SPICED CITRUS DRESSING IS ABSOLUTELY DELICIOUS.

500 g (1 lb) sweet potatoes, sliced
3 tablespoons olive oil
250 g (8 oz) haloumi cheese, patted dry on kitchen paper
75 g (3 oz) rocket leaves

Dressing
5 tablespoons olive oil
3 tablespoons clear honey
2 tablespoons lemon or lime juice
1½ teaspoons black onion seeds
1 red chilli, deseeded and finely sliced
2 teaspoons chopped lemon thyme
salt and pepper

Serves **4**
Prep time **10 minutes**
Cooking time **15 minutes**

1 Mix together all the ingredients for the dressing in a small bowl.

2 Cook the sweet potatoes in a saucepan of lightly salted boiling water for 2 minutes. Drain well. Heat the oil in a large frying pan, add the sweet potatoes and fry for about 10 minutes, turning once, until golden.

3 Meanwhile, thinly slice the cheese and place on a lightly oiled foil-lined grill rack. Cook under a preheated medium grill for about 3 minutes until golden.

4 Pile the sweet potatoes, cheese and rocket on to serving plates and spoon over the dressing.

PANZANELLA

FOR THIS SALAD, IT IS BEST TO USE SLIGHTLY STALE CIABATTA THAT WILL NOT FALL APART. ALTERNATIVELY, USE LIGHTLY TOASTED FRESH BREAD.

3 red peppers, cored, deseeded and quartered
375 g (12 oz) ripe plum tomatoes, skinned
6 tablespoons olive oil
3 tablespoons wine vinegar
2 garlic cloves, crushed
125 g (4 oz) stale ciabatta bread
50 g (2 oz) pitted black olives
small handful of basil leaves, shredded
salt and pepper

Serves **4**
Prep time **20 minutes**
Cooking time **10 minutes**

1 Place the peppers, skin side up, on a foil-lined grill rack and grill under a preheated medium grill for 10 minutes or until the skins are blackened.

2 Meanwhile, quarter the tomatoes and scoop out the pulp, placing it in a sieve over a bowl to catch the juices. Set the tomato quarters aside. Press the pulp with the back of a spoon to extract as much juice as possible.

3 Beat the oil, vinegar, garlic and salt and pepper into the tomato juice.

4 When cool enough to handle, peel the skins from the peppers and discard. Roughly slice the peppers and place in a bowl with the tomato quarters. Break the bread into small chunks and add to the bowl with the olives and basil.

5 Add the dressing and toss the ingredients together before serving.

WARM AUBERGINE SALAD

2 tablespoons olive oil
2 aubergines, cut into small cubes
1 red onion, finely sliced
2 tablespoons capers, drained and roughly chopped
4 tomatoes, chopped
4 tablespoons chopped parsley
1 tablespoon balsamic vinegar
salt and pepper

Serves **4**
Prep time **10 minutes, plus cooling**
Cooking time **10 minutes**

1 Heat the oil in a nonstick frying pan, add the aubergines and fry for 10 minutes until golden and softened.

2 Add the onion, capers, tomatoes, parsley and vinegar and stir to combine. Season lightly to taste. Remove from the heat and leave to cool for 10 minutes before serving.

COOKING TIP

Don't throw away the last few pasta shapes in the packet: collect them in a food container and you'll have an eclectic mix for your next pasta dinner. Most regular pasta shapes cook at roughly the same time so you shouldn't need to worry about cooking times.

Warm Pasta Salad WITH LEMON & BROCCOLI

1 Cook the pasta in a large saucepan of lightly salted boiling water according to the pack instructions, adding the broccoli florets, soya beans, peas and sugar snaps for the final 3 minutes of the cooking time. Drain the pasta and vegetables, reserving a ladleful of the cooking water, then return to the pan.

2 Stir in the soft cheese, lemon rind and juice, olive oil, chilli, grated cheese, tarragon, some salt and pepper and a splash of cooking water. Serve the salad warm or at room temperature.

375 g (12 oz) dried penne or rigatoni
150 g (5 oz) broccoli florets
100 g (3½ oz) frozen soya beans
100 g (3½ oz) frozen peas
100 g (3½ oz) sugar snap peas, trimmed
150 g (5 oz) soft cheese with garlic and herbs
finely grated rind and juice of 1 lemon
4 tablespoons olive oil
1 red chilli, deseeded and finely chopped
100 g (3½ oz) grated Parmesan-style cheese
2 tablespoons chopped tarragon leaves
salt and pepper

Serves **4**
Prep time **10 minutes**
Cooking time **10-12 minutes**

MUSHROOM & EGG Fried Rice

2 tablespoons vegetable oil
200 g (7 oz) mushrooms, chopped
2 spring onions
1 large egg, beaten
250 g (8 oz) cooked rice
soy sauce, to serve

Serves **2**
Prep time **5 minutes**
Cooking time **10 minutes**

1 Heat the oil in a large frying pan, add the mushrooms and spring onions and stir-fry over a medium heat for 4–5 minutes until the mushrooms have softened.

2 Increase the heat and add the beaten egg to the pan. Cook for a further 2 minutes, stirring frequently, until the egg is cooked.

3 Stir in the rice and heat until it is piping hot, then serve immediately with soy sauce.

STUDENT TIP

If you have a strict food budget, only take the exact amount of cash you have to spend when you go shopping. That way you won't be tempted to top up your trolley with unnecessary luxuries and pile it on the credit card when you get to the checkout.

TABBOULEH with Fruit & Nuts

IF PRUNES ARE NOT YOUR FAVOURITE DRIED FRUIT, SUBSTITUTE JUST ABOUT ANY OTHER – APRICOTS, PLUMP SULTANAS OR RAISINS. FIGS AND DATES ARE ALSO GOOD.

150 g (5 oz) bulgar wheat
75 g (3 oz) unsalted, shelled pistachio nuts
1 small red onion, finely chopped
3 garlic cloves, crushed
25 g (1 oz) flat leaf parsley, chopped
15 g (½ oz) mint, chopped
finely grated rind and juice of 1 lemon or lime
150 g (5 oz) ready-to-eat prunes, sliced
4 tablespoons olive oil
salt and pepper

Serves **4**
Prep time **15 minutes, plus soaking**

1 Place the bulgar wheat in a bowl, cover with plenty of boiling water and leave for 15 minutes.

2 Meanwhile, place the pistachio nuts in a separate bowl and cover with boiling water. Leave to stand for 1 minute, then drain. Rub the nuts between several thicknesses of kitchen paper to remove most of the skins, then peel away any remaining skins with your fingers.

3 Mix the nuts with the onion, garlic, parsley, mint, lemon or lime rind and juice and prunes in a large bowl.

4 Drain the bulgar wheat thoroughly in a sieve, pressing out as much moisture as possible with the back of a spoon. Add to the other ingredients with the oil and toss together. Season to taste with salt and pepper and chill until ready to serve.

Sweet Potato & GARLIC MASH

1 Place the sweet potatoes and smoked garlic cloves in a large saucepan, cover with cold water and bring to the boil. Reduce the heat and simmer for 10–12 minutes until tender, then drain well. Return the sweet potatoes and garlic to the pan and mash until smooth.

2 Set the pan over a low heat, then push the mash to one side, add the butter to the base of the pan and leave to melt. Pour the milk on to the butter and heat for 1–2 minutes, then beat into the mash.

3 Stir in the parsley, season to taste with salt and pepper and serve.

1 kg (2 lb) sweet potatoes, peeled and cut into 2.5 cm (1 inch) pieces
4–6 smoked garlic cloves, peeled but left whole
25 g (1 oz) salted butter
2 tablespoons milk
2 tablespoons chopped flat leaf parsley
salt and pepper

Serves **4**
Prep time **10 minutes**
Cooking time **15–20 minutes**

BAKED SWEET POTATOES

4 sweet potatoes, about 250 g (8 oz) each, scrubbed
200 g (7 oz) soured cream
2 spring onions, trimmed and finely chopped
1 tablespoon chopped chives
50 g (2 oz) butter
salt and pepper

Serves 4
Prep time 5 minutes
Cooking time 45-50 minutes

1 Put the potatoes in a roasting tin and roast in a preheated oven, 220°C (425°F), Gas Mark 7, for 45-50 minutes until cooked through.

2 Meanwhile, combine the soured cream, spring onions, chives and salt and pepper in a bowl.

3 Cut the baked potatoes in half lengthways, top with the butter and spoon over the soured cream mixture. Serve immediately.

Crisp Parsnip CAKES

750 g (1½ lb) parsnips, peeled and chopped
50 g (2 oz) butter
1 garlic clove, crushed
1 tablespoon chopped thyme
flour, for dusting
2 tablespoons vegetable oil
salt and pepper

Serves 4
Prep time 10 minutes, plus cooling
Cooking time 20–25 minutes

1 Cook the parsnips in a large saucepan of lightly salted boiling water for 10 minutes until tender.

2 Meanwhile, melt the butter in a small frying pan, add the garlic and thyme and cook gently, stirring, for 2 minutes.

3 Drain the parsnips, return to the pan and mash thoroughly. Mash in the buttery garlic mixture and season well with salt and pepper. Leave until cool enough to handle. Shape the parsnip mixture into 8 patties with lightly floured hands.

4 Heat 1 tablespoon of the oil in a large frying pan, add 4 of the patties and cook for 3–4 minutes on each side until golden brown. Transfer the patties to a baking sheet and keep warm in a low oven while you repeat with the remaining oil and patties. Serve warm.

Corn & Courgette Cakes

1 Place the corn in a large bowl with the courgette, cumin seeds, spring onions, flour, eggs, coriander, chilli and some salt and pepper and mix well.

2 Heat 1 tablespoon of the oil in a large nonstick frying pan and cook spoonfuls of the mixture in batches for 2–3 minutes on each side until cooked through. Drain on kitchen paper and keep warm while cooking the remainder in the same way; the mixture makes 12 cakes.

3 Serve with guacamole and lime wedges.

150 g (5 oz) fresh sweetcorn kernels
1 courgette, coarsely grated
1 teaspoon cumin seeds
4 spring onions, thinly sliced
3 tablespoons self-raising flour
2 eggs, beaten
2 tablespoons chopped fresh coriander
1 red chilli, deseeded and roughly chopped
vegetable oil, for frying
salt and pepper

To serve
ready-made guacamole
lime wedges

Serves **4**
Prep time **10 minutes,**
Cooking time **15-20 minutes**

CHARGRILLED POLENTA TRIANGLES

olive oil, for brushing
2 teaspoons salt
175 g (6 oz) instant polenta
2 garlic cloves, crushed
50 g (2 oz) butter
50 g (2 oz) Parmesan-style cheese, grated, plus extra to serve
pepper
chopped fresh parsley, to garnish

Serves **4**
Prep time **5 minutes, plus cooling**
Cooking time **20–25 minutes**

AFFORDABILITY 1

1 Lightly brush a 23 x 30 cm (9 x 12 inch) baking tin with oil. Bring 1 litre ($1\frac{3}{4}$ pints) water to the boil in a heavy-based saucepan, add the salt and then gradually whisk in the polenta in a steady stream. Cook over a low heat, stirring constantly with a wooden spoon, for 5 minutes until the grains have swelled and thickened. Remove from the heat and immediately beat in the garlic, butter, cheese and pepper until smooth. Pour the mixture into the tin and leave to cool.

2 Turn the polenta out on to a chopping board and cut into large squares, then diagonally in half into triangles. Brush the triangles with a little oil.

3 Heat a large frying pan, or ridged griddle pan if you have one, until hot. Add the polenta triangles, in batches, and cook over a medium-high heat for 2–3 minutes on each side until charred and heated through. Serve immediately, sprinkled with grated cheese and chopped parsley.

Mustard RAREBIT

1 Heat the butter in a frying pan, add the spring onions and fry for 5 minutes or until softened.

2 Reduce the heat to low and stir in the cheese, beer and mustard. Season well with pepper, then stir slowly for 3-4 minutes or until the cheese has melted.

3 Meanwhile, toast the bread lightly on both sides and place on a grill pan. Pour the cheese mixture over the toast and cook under a preheated hot grill for 1 minute or until bubbling and golden. Serve with lettuce, radishes and tomatoes.

25 g (1 oz) butter
4 spring onions, thinly sliced
250 g (8 oz) Cheddar or Red Leicester cheese, grated
50 ml (2 fl oz) beer
2 teaspoons mustard
4 slices of wholemeal bread
pepper

To serve
Little Gem lettuce leaves
cherry tomatoes
radishes

Serves **4**
Prep time **5 minutes**
Cooking time **10 minutes**

GARLIC & BEAN PÂTÉ

425 g (14 oz) can flageolet beans, rinsed and drained
125 g (4 oz) cream cheese
2 garlic cloves, chopped
3 tablespoons homemade (see page 249) or ready-made pesto
2 spring onions, chopped
1 tablespoon olive oil
salt and pepper

To serve
cucumber sticks
pitta breads

Serves **4**
Prep time **5 minutes**

1 Using a stick blender, or a food processor or blender if you have one, whizz the beans, cream cheese, garlic and 2 tablespoons of the pesto until smooth. Add the spring onions and salt and pepper to taste and blend for 10 seconds.

2 Spoon into a dish and chill until required. Mix the remaining pesto with the olive oil and drizzle on top before serving with cucumber sticks and lightly toasted pitta breads cut into thick strips.

RED CABBAGE & BEETROOT LENTILS

2 tablespoons vegetable oil
½ small red cabbage, thinly sliced
2 spring onions, sliced, plus extra to garnish
1 beetroot, coarsely grated
1 teaspoon ground cumin
300 g (10 oz) canned green lentils, rinsed and drained
salt and pepper
natural or Greek yogurt, to serve

Serves **2**
Prep time **5 minutes**
Cooking time **15–20 minutes**

1 Heat the oil in a saucepan, add the red cabbage and spring onions and cook over a medium heat for about 5 minutes until just beginning to soften. Stir in the beetroot, then cover with a lid and cook for a further 8–10 minutes, stirring occasionally, until the vegetables are tender.

2 Sprinkle over the ground cumin and stir over the heat for a minute, then add the lentils and heat until hot. Season to taste, then serve with dollops of yogurt and extra sliced spring onions.

RED CABBAGE COLESLAW

1 In a bowl, combine the red cabbage, beetroot and apple.

2 In a separate small bowl or jar, whisk together the dressing ingredients.

3 Pour the dressing over the coleslaw and mix well to coat. Serve with warmed wholemeal pittas.

½ small red cabbage, thinly sliced
1 small beetroot, coarsely grated
1 small dessert apple, peeled, cored and coarsely grated
warm wholemeal pitta breads, to serve

Dressing
1 tablespoon wholegrain mustard
1 spring onion, finely chopped
2 teaspoons red wine vinegar
2 tablespoons olive oil

Serves **2**
Prep time **10 minutes**

STUDENT TIP

Although it's sometimes difficult to tell which fruit and vegetables are in season, if you shop according to the season your food bill will be less. Local markets are a good place to start – the produce needs to be harvested when it's ready and sold quickly so take advantage!

POTATO TORTILLA

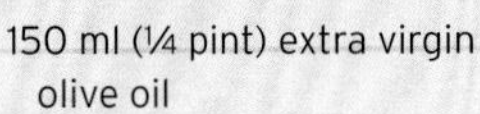

150 ml (¼ pint) extra virgin olive oil
750 g (1½ lb) waxy potatoes, thinly sliced
1 onion, chopped
1 red pepper, deseeded and sliced
1 green pepper, sliced
5 eggs, beaten
salt and pepper

Serves **6**
Prep time **10 minutes, plus standing**
Cooking time **30-35 minutes**

1 Heat all but 2 tablespoons of the oil in a large nonstick frying pan and fry the potatoes, onion and peppers, stirring frequently, for 15 minutes, until all the vegetables are golden and tender.

2 Mix the potato mixture with the eggs in a large bowl and season well with salt and pepper. Set aside for 15 minutes. Clean the frying pan.

3 Heat the remaining oil in the clean pan and tip in the tortilla mixture. Cook over a low heat for 10 minutes, until almost cooked through. Carefully slide the tortilla onto a large plate, invert the frying pan over the tortilla and then flip it back into the frying pan.

4 Return the pan to the heat and cook the tortilla for a further 5 minutes, or until it is cooked on both sides. Leave to cool, then serve at room temperature, cut into wedges.

CHUNKY POTATO CHIPS

1 kg (2 lb) baking potatoes
150 ml (¼ pint) mild olive oil or groundnut oil
1 teaspoon paprika
1 teaspoon celery salt
salt and pepper

Serves **4**
Prep time **10 minutes**
Cooking time **50 minutes**

1 Cut the potatoes into 1 cm (½ inch) slices, then cut each slice into chunky chips.

2 Brush a large roasting tin with a little of the oil and heat it in a preheated oven, 220°C (425°F), Gas Mark 7, for 5 minutes.

3 Scatter the chips in the tin, drizzle with the remaining oil and sprinkle with the paprika and celery salt. Mix until well coated and bake for 45 minutes, turning the chips occasionally, until they are golden. Serve sprinkled with salt and pepper.

What's for Afters?

CHOCOLATE FRIDGE CAKE

BANOFFEE LAYERS

210 INSTANT SUMMER BERRY SORBET
211 FROZEN FRUIT PUDDING
212 SUMMER FRUITS WITH HONEYED OAT TOPPING
213 STRAWBERRY CRUSH
214 NUTTY PASSIONFRUIT YOGURTS
215 BANOFFEE LAYERS
216 MANGO & MINT CARPACCIO
218 PINEAPPLE WITH LIME & CHILLI SYRUP
219 CHOCOLATE FROMAGE FRAIS
220 QUICK TIRAMISU
221 ALMOST INSTANT PEACH TRIFLE
222 CHOCOLATE FRIDGE CAKE
223 RICH CHOCOLATE MOUSSE
224 STRAWBERRY CHEESECAKE MUG CAKE
225 TREACLE SPONGE MICROWAVE PUDDINGS
226 TOFFEE APPLE BAKE
227 SYRUPY PEARS WITH CHOCOLATE CRUMBLE
228 WARM SPICED PLUMS
229 FRUITY BAKED APPLES
230 RHUBARB & RASPBERRY CRUMBLE
232 SWEET & STICKY RAISIN PUDDING
233 CHOC CINNAMON EGGY BREAD

STRAWBERRY CRUSH

Instant Summer BERRY SORBET

300 g (10 oz) frozen summer berries
400 ml (14 fl oz) raspberry yogurt
6 tablespoons icing sugar

Serves 4
Prep time 5 minutes

1 Using a stick blender, or a food processor or blender if you have one available, whizz the frozen berries, yogurt and sugar until blended.

2 Scrape the mixture from the sides of the bowl and blend together again.

3 Spoon into chilled glasses or bowls and serve immediately.

Frozen Fruit PUDDING

1 Grease a 20 x 25 cm (8 x 10 inch) shallow ovenproof dish, then tip in the frozen fruit with 50 g (2 oz) of the sugar.

2 Beat together the remaining sugar, butter or margarine, eggs and flour in a bowl until smooth. Spoon the mixture over the frozen fruit and smooth down evenly.

3 Bake in a preheated oven, 200°C (400°F), Gas Mark 6, for 20–25 minutes until risen and golden, then serve with vanilla ice cream, if liked.

125 g (4 oz) butter or margarine, softened, plus extra for greasing
500 g (1 lb) mixed frozen fruit
175 g (6 oz) caster sugar
2 eggs
125 g (4 oz) self-raising flour
vanilla ice cream, to serve (optional)

Serves **4–6**
Prep time **10 minutes**
Cooking time **20–25 minutes**

SUMMER FRUITS WITH HONEYED OAT TOPPING

1 Put the apricots and strawberries in a bowl. Add the Greek yogurt and honey and sprinkle the oats and almonds over the top.

4 apricots, halved and stoned
4 strawberries, hulled and halved
1 dessertspoon clear honey
1 tablespoon Greek yogurt
1 tablespoon medium rolled oats
1 tablespoon toasted almonds

Serves **1**
Prep time **5 minutes**

COOKING TIP

Use freezer stickers to record the food and the date. You'll be pleased you made the effort in a few months' time when you're hungry but have no idea what the bag of frozen mush is at the back of the freezer, or how long it's been there.

Strawberry CRUSH

- 400 g (13 oz) strawberries, hulled
- 1 tablespoon icing sugar
- 300 g (10 oz) low-fat fromage frais
- 4 ready-made meringue nests
- 4 lavender sprigs, to decorate (optional)

Serves **4**
Prep time **5 minutes**

1 Using a fork, or a food processor or blender if you have one, mash the strawberries with the icing sugar.

2 Put the fromage frais in a bowl, crumble in the meringues and mix together lightly.

3 Add the strawberry mixture and fold together with a spoon until marbled. Spoon into glasses and serve decorated with lavender sprigs, if using.

NUTTY PASSIONFRUIT YOGURTS

1 Halve the passionfruit and scoop the pulp into a large bowl. Add the yogurt and mix together gently.

2 Put 1 tablespoonful of honey in the bottom of each of two narrow glasses and scatter over a few hazelnuts. Spoon half the yogurt over the nuts and arrange half the clementine pieces on top.

3 Repeat the layering, finishing with a few hazelnuts on the top of the dish. Chill until ready to serve.

2 passionfruit
250 ml (8 fl oz) natural yogurt
2 tablespoons clear honey
25 g (1 oz) hazelnuts, roughly chopped
4 clementines, peeled and chopped into small pieces

Serves 2
Prep time **5 minutes**

BANOFFEE LAYERS

6 digestive biscuits, crushed
2 large bananas
50 g (2 oz) butter
50 g (2 oz) soft dark brown sugar
150 ml (¼ pint) double cream
200 ml (7 fl oz) crème fraîche
grated plain dark chocolate, to decorate

Serves 4
Prep time 10 minutes
Cooking time 5 minutes

1 Divide the biscuit crumbs among four tall serving glasses and use to line each base. Mash one of the bananas and divide among the glasses, spooning on top of the biscuit crumbs.

2 Melt the butter in a small saucepan, add the sugar and heat over a medium heat, stirring well, until the sugar has dissolved. Add the cream and cook gently for 1–2 minutes until the mixture is thick. Remove from the heat and leave to cool for 1 minute, then spoon on top of the mashed banana.

3 Slice the second banana and arrange on top of the caramel, then spoon over the crème fraîche. Decorate with grated plain dark chocolate before serving.

MANGO & MINT (V)
Carpaccio

6 tablespoons caster sugar
finely grated rind and juice of 1 large lime
2 tablespoons finely chopped mint leaves, plus extra leaves to decorate
4 firm, ripe mangoes

Serves **4**
Prep time **10 minutes, plus cooling**
Cooking time **5 minutes**

1 Put the sugar in a small saucepan with the lime rind and juice, mint and 6–8 tablespoons water. Bring to the boil and remove from the heat. Stir until the sugar is dissolved. Leave to cool.

2 Meanwhile, cut the mangoes in half, running a sharp knife around the stones to detach. Peel and slice as thinly as possible.

3 Arrange the mango slices on serving plates and drizzle with the sugar syrup. Serve decorated with mint leaves.

V

PINEAPPLE WITH LIME & CHILLI SYRUP

100 g (3½ oz) caster sugar
3 red chillies, deseeded and finely diced
grated rind and juice of 1 lime
1 small pineapple, halved or quartered, cored and cut into wafer-thin slices

Serves **4**
Prep time **10 minutes, plus cooling**
Cooking time **10 minutes**

1 Put the sugar and 100 ml (3½ fl oz) water in a saucepan and heat slowly until the sugar has dissolved, then add the chillies, bring to the boil and boil rapidly until the liquid becomes syrupy. Leave to cool.

2 Stir the lime rind and juice into the cooled syrup. Lay the pineapple slices on a plate and drizzle the syrup over. Serve chilled.

CHOCOLATE FROMAGE FRAIS

300 g (10 oz) plain dark
chocolate, broken up
500 g (1 lb) fromage frais
1 teaspoon vanilla extract

Serves 6
Prep time 5 minutes

1 Melt the chocolate in a heatproof bowl set over a pan of simmering water (do not let the bowl touch the water), then remove from the heat. Add the fromage frais and vanilla extract and quickly stir together.

2 Divide the chocolate fromage frais among little pots or glasses and serve immediately.

QUICK Tiramisu

5 tablespoons strong espresso coffee
75 g (3 oz) dark muscovado sugar
4 tablespoons coffee liqueur or 3 tablespoons brandy
75 g (3 oz) sponge finger biscuits, broken into large pieces
400 g (13 oz) ready-made custard
250 g (8 oz) mascarpone cheese
1 teaspoon vanilla extract
50 g (2 oz) plain dark chocolate, finely chopped
cocoa powder, for dusting

Serves **4–6**
Prep time **15 minutes, plus chilling**

1 Mix the coffee with 2 tablespoons of the sugar and the liqueur or brandy in a medium bowl. Toss the sponge fingers in the mixture and turn into a serving dish, spooning over any excess liquid.

2 Beat together the custard, mascarpone and vanilla extract and spoon a third over the biscuits. Sprinkle with the remaining sugar, then half the remaining custard. Scatter with the chopped chocolate, then spread with the remaining custard.

3 Chill for about 1 hour until set and serve lightly dusted with cocoa powder.

Almost Instant PEACH TRIFLE

175 g (6 oz) raspberry Swiss roll, sliced
400 g (13 oz) can sliced peaches in juice, drained, juice reserved
200 g (7 oz) mascarpone cheese
200 g (7 oz) ready-made custard
2 tablespoons icing sugar
150 ml (¼ pint) double cream, whipped
25 g (1 oz) plain dark chocolate, grated, to decorate

Serves **4**
Prep time **10 minutes**

1 Line the base of a glass serving dish with the Swiss roll slices. Drizzle over 100 ml (3½ fl oz) of the reserved juice, then scatter over the sliced peaches.

2 Beat the mascarpone with the custard and icing sugar, then spoon it over the fruit.

3 Spoon the whipped cream over the custard, then decorate with the grated chocolate.

Chocolate FRIDGE CAKE

AS DELICIOUS AS IT IS FILLING, THIS ISN'T THE SORT OF CAKE YOU'D SERVE IN CHUNKY SLICES. RICH AND INTENSELY CHOCOLATEY, IT'S A TREAT CUT INTO SMALL PIECES AND SERVED WITH COFFEE.

300 g (10 oz) plain dark chocolate, broken up
75 g (3 oz) unsalted butter
125 g (4 oz) bought or homemade shortbread biscuits, broken into small pieces
125 g (4 oz) whole mixed nuts, such as almonds, hazelnuts and Brazil nuts
150 g (5 oz) milk chocolate caramel bar, broken into sections

Makes **10 pieces**
Prep time **10 minutes, plus chilling**

1 Line a dampened 500 g (1 lb) loaf tin with clingfilm. Melt the plain chocolate with the butter in a heatproof bowl set over a pan of simmering water (do not let the bowl touch the water), stirring frequently, then leave until cool but not beginning to harden.

2 Stir the biscuits, nuts and caramel bar into the melted mixture until combined. Turn into the tin and pack down in an even layer. Chill for several hours or overnight until set.

3 To serve, lift away the tin and let the cake softren a little at room temperature so it's easier to slice. Peel away the clingfilm and serve in small pieces.

RICH CHOCOLATE MOUSSE

1 Melt the chocolate with the cream in a heatproof bowl set over a pan of simmering water (do not let the bowl touch the water), stirring frequently, until smooth. Leave to cool for 5 minutes, then beat in the egg yolks one at a time.

2 Whisk the egg whites in a separate clean bowl until stiff, then lightly fold into the chocolate mixture until combined. Spoon the mousse into glasses or cups and chill for 2 hours. Dust with cocoa powder before serving.

175 g (6 oz) plain dark chocolate, broken into pieces
100 ml (3 fl oz) double cream
3 eggs, separated
cocoa powder, for dusting

Serves **4**
Prep time **10 minutes, plus chilling**

Strawberry Cheesecake MUG CAKE

75 g (3 oz) cream cheese
2 teaspoons caster sugar
1 egg yolk
2 tablespoons single cream or milk
2 teaspoons strawberry conserve or jam
handful of strawberries, hulled and halved, to serve
1 gingersnap biscuit, crushed

Serves 1
Prep time **5 minutes, plus cooling**
Cooking time **2 minutes**

1 Choose a small microwave-proof mug with a capacity of at least 175ml (6 fl oz). You can test whether a mug is suitable for the microwave by filling it with cold water and microwaving on full power for 1 minute. If the water heats up but the mug doesn't get hot it's fine to use.

2 Put the cream cheese and sugar in the mug and beat with a small whisk or spoon until the cream cheese softens. Beat in the egg yolk and cream or milk.

3 Dot the conserve or jam over the surface. Cut through the jam with a knife several times so it is marbled into the cream cheese without being completely blended. Microwave on medium power for 1 minute. The edges of the cheesecake will be set while the centre is very loose. If the edges haven't set, return the mug to the microwave for a further 15-30 seconds. Leave to cool.

4 Pile the strawberries on top of the cheesecake and scatter with the biscuit crumbs to serve.

Treacle Sponge MICROWAVE PUDDINGS

100 g (3½ oz) butter, softened, plus extra for greasing
100 g (3½ oz) soft light brown sugar
100 g (3½ oz) self-raising flour
1 teaspoon mixed spice
1 egg, beaten
4 tablespoons golden syrup
custard, to serve

Serves **4**
Prep time **10 minutes**
Cooking time **5–7 minutes**

1 Lightly grease four 150 ml (¼ pint) ramekins and line the bases with nonstick baking paper. Beat together the butter and sugar in a bowl until pale and fluffy, then sift in the flour and spice and add the egg. Beat together until well mixed.

2 Divide the mixture among the ramekins. Cover each with a disc of baking paper and cook together in a microwave on high for 2–2½ minutes, then leave the sponges to rest for 3–4 minutes to finish cooking.

3 Turn the puddings out on to a serving plates and drizzle each with 1 tablespoon of the golden syrup while still warm. Serve with custard.

Toffee Apple Bake

1 Toss the apples in a shallow ovenproof dish with the 1 tablespoon flour and the muscovado sugar.

2 Mix the remaining flour with the caster sugar and spice in a bowl. Add the egg, yogurt and butter and stir lightly until only just combined.

3 Spoon the mixture over the apples and bake in a preheated oven, 220°C (425°F), Gas Mark 7, for about 15–20 minutes until just firm and golden. Serve warm.

3 dessert apples, cored and thickly sliced
100 g (3½ oz) self-raising flour, plus 1 tablespoon extra
125 g (4 oz) light muscovado sugar
50 g (2 oz) caster sugar
½ teaspoon ground mixed spice
1 egg
100 ml (3½ fl oz) natural yogurt
50 g (2 oz) unsalted butter, melted

Serves **4**
Prep time **10 minutes**
Cooking time **15–20 minutes**

STUDENT TIP
Ditch the takeaways and cook your own curry: you'll need a few basic spices and vegetarian curry pastes to start off your storecupboard, but after that you'll save a fortune every time you cook your own instead of dialling for a takeout.

SYRUPY PEARS
with chocolate crumble

1 Place half of the sugar in a frying pan with 150 ml (¼ pint) water and the raisins and cinnamon. Bring just to the boil, add the pears and simmer gently, uncovered, for about 5 minutes until the pears are slightly softened.

2 Meanwhile, melt the butter in a separate frying pan or saucepan, add the porridge oats and fry gently for 2 minutes. Stir in the remaining sugar and cook over a gentle heat until golden.

3 Spoon the pears on to warmed serving plates. Stir the hazelnuts and chocolate into the oats mixture. Once the chocolate starts to melt, spoon over the pears. Serve topped with whipped cream or Greek yogurt, if liked.

50 g (2 oz) light muscovado sugar
25 g (1 oz) raisins
½ teaspoon ground cinnamon
4 ripe dessert pears, peeled, halved and cored
40 g (1½ oz) unsalted butter
50 g (2 oz) porridge oats
25 g (1 oz) hazelnuts, roughly chopped
50 g (2 oz) plain or milk chocolate, chopped
lightly whipped cream or Greek yogurt, to serve (optional)

Serves **4**
Prep time **5 minutes**
Cooking time **10 minutes**

WARM SPICED PLUMS

1 Place the plums, sugar, spices and 3 tablespoons water in a large, heavy-based saucepan and bring to the boil, stirring occasionally.

2 Reduce the heat to low, cover with a lid and simmer very gently for 15–20 minutes, stirring occasionally, until the plums are tender. Transfer to a large serving dish and leave to cool for 5 minutes before serving with scoops of ice cream.

750 g (1½ lb) ripe plums, halved and stoned
100 g (3½ oz) caster sugar
½ teaspoon ground cinnamon
½ teaspoon ground ginger
vanilla ice cream, to serve

Serves **4**
Prep time **5 minutes**
Cooking time **20–25 minutes**

Fruity BAKED APPLES V

4 large dessert apples
125 g (4 oz) ready-to-eat dried fruit, such as cranberries, sultanas and apricots
4 teaspoons demerara sugar

Serves 4
Prep time **5 minutes**
Cooking time **25 minutes**

1 Core the apples and score a line around the middle of the fruit and arrange them in an ovenproof dish. Stuff the cored centre of the apples with the dried fruit.

2 Sprinkle over the sugar and bake in a preheated oven, 200°C (400°F), Gas Mark 6, for 25 minutes or until the apples are tender.

Rhubarb & Raspberry CRUMBLE

500 g (1 lb) fresh or frozen rhubarb (thawed if frozen), sliced
125 g (4 oz) fresh or frozen raspberries
50 g (2 oz) soft light brown sugar
3 tablespoons orange juice
raspberry ripple ice cream, to serve

Crumble topping
200 g (7 oz) plain flour
pinch of salt
150 g (5 oz) cold unsalted butter, diced, plus extra for greasing
50 g (2 oz) soft light brown sugar

Serves **4**
Prep time **10 minutes**
Cooking time **25 minutes**

1 Make the crumble topping. Place the flour and salt in a bowl, add the butter and rub in with the fingertips until the mixture resembles breadcrumbs. Stir in the sugar.

2 Mix the fruits, sugar and orange juice together in a separate bowl, then tip into a greased ovenproof dish. Sprinkle over the topping and bake in a preheated oven, 200°C (400°F), Gas Mark 6, for about 25 minutes or until golden brown and bubbling. Serve the crumble hot with raspberry ripple ice cream.

SWEET & STICKY RAISIN PUDDING

1 Grease a 20 x 25 cm (8 x 10 inch) shallow ovenproof dish, then pour in the golden syrup.

2 Beat the remaining ingredients together until pale and creamy and spoon over the syrup base. Bake in a preheated oven, 200°C (400°F), Gas Mark 6, for 20–25 minutes or until risen and golden. Serve with cream or custard, if liked.

125 g (4 oz) butter, softened, plus extra for greasing
6 tablespoons golden syrup
125 g (4 oz) self-raising flour
125 g (4 oz) caster sugar
2 large eggs
1 teaspoon vanilla extract (optional)
75 g (3 oz) raisins
single cream or custard, to serve (optional)

Serves **6**
Prep time **5 minutes**
Cooking time **20–25 minutes**

STUDENT TIP

Now that most big supermarkets seem to be open 24/7, it's not as easy to pick up a closing-time bargain as it used to be. But if you hang around near the end of the day you can still grab some good deals – just make sure you buy food that you are actually going to eat.

Choc Cinnamon EGGY BREAD

- 2 eggs, lightly beaten
- 2 thick slices of seeded brown bread, cut in half
- 15 g (½ oz) butter
- 2 tablespoons caster sugar
- 2 teaspoons cocoa powder
- ½ teaspoon ground cinnamon

Serves **2**
Prep time **5 minutes**
Cooking time **4 minutes**

1 Place the eggs in a shallow dish. Press the bread into the egg mixture, turning to coat well.

2 Melt the butter in a heavy-based pan and add the eggy bread. Cook for 3 minutes, turning as needed.

3 Mix the sugar, cocoa powder and cinnamon on a plate and place the hot eggy bread on top, turning to coat. Serve immediately.

236 PIMM'S COCKTAIL
236 SANGRIA
237 MOJITO
238 WHITE RUSSIAN
238 COSMOPOLITAN
239 TEQUILA SUNRISE LOLLIPOPS
242 CARROT, CHILLI & PINEAPPLE JUICE
242 MIXED BERRY SMOOTHIE
243 CRANBERRY & APPLE SMOOTHIE
243 CLASSIC LEMONADE
244 ORANGE & RASPBERRY JUICE
244 APPLE, APRICOT & PEACH JUICE
245 FRUITY SUMMER MILKSHAKE
245 BANANA LASSI
246 VEGETABLE STOCK
246 VEGGIE GRAVY
247 TOMATO SAUCE
247 BÉCHAMEL SAUCE
248 RICH CHEESE SAUCE
248 PARSLEY SAUCE
249 PESTO
250 APPLE SAUCE
250 GLOSSY CHOCOLATE SAUCE
251 BUTTERCREAM
251 CREAM CHEESE FROSTING

CARROT, CHILLI & PINEAPPLE JUICE

Bar, Drinks & Basics

MIXED BERRY SMOOTHIE

TEQUILA SUNRISE LOLLIPOPS

PIMM'S COCKTAIL

ice cubes
1 measure Pimm's No 1
1 measure gin
2 measures lemonade
2 measures ginger ale
cucumber strips, blueberries and orange wheels, to decorate

Serves **1**
Prep time **3 minutes**

1 Fill a tall glass with ice cubes. Pour all the remaining ingredients, one by one in order, over the ice.

2 Decorate with cucumber strips, blueberries and orange wheels and serve.

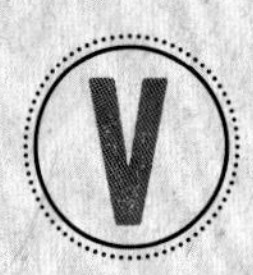

SANGRIA

ice cubes
6 measures Spanish brandy
8 measures fresh orange juice
500 ml (17 fl oz) red wine
1 litre (1¾ pints) soda water or lemonade, to top up
orange slices and cinnamon sticks, to decorate

Serves **6**
Prep time **5 minutes**

1 Put a small number of ice cubes in a large jug. Pour over the brandy, orange juice and wine and stir well.

2 Add more ice, top up with soda water or lemonade and decorate with orange slices and cinnamon sticks. Serve in ice-filled wine glasses.

MOJITO

THIS IS A COOLING, EFFERVESCENT COCKTAIL BORN – THANKS TO PROHIBITION – AMID CUBA'S THRIVING INTERNATIONAL BAR CULTURE. IT PROBABLY DERIVED FROM THE MINT JULEP.

12 mint leaves, plus an extra sprig to decorate
½ measure sugar syrup (see page 243)
4 lime wedges
crushed ice
2 measures white rum
soda water, to top up

Serves 1
Prep time 2 minutes

1 Put the mint, sugar syrup and lime wedges into a tall glass and muddle together (see below).

2 Fill the glass with crushed ice, pour over the rum and stir. Top up with soda water. Decorate with a mint sprig and serve with straws.

TECHNIQUE: *Muddling*

This is used to bring out the flavours of fruit and herbs using a muddler (the rounded end of a wooden spoon handle works too). A famous example is the Mojito, where mint, sugar syrup and lime wedges are muddled in the bottom of a tall glass before the remaining ingredients are added.

Remove the mint leaves from their stems and put them into the bottom of a tall glass.

Add the sugar syrup and lime wedges. Hold the glass firmly with one hand and use the muddler to press down on the mint and lime wedges. Twist the muddler and press firmly to release the flavour of the mint and to break it down with the juice from the lime wedges. Continue this process for about 30 seconds, then top up the glass with crushed ice. Add the remaining ingredients to the glass, as specified in the recipe.

White RUSSIAN

THIS MODERN TAKE ON THE BLACK RUSSIAN USES TIA MARIA AND CREAM TO GIVE THE DRINK ITS DISTINCTIVE COLOUR AND TEXTURE.

6 ice cubes, cracked
1 measure vodka
1 measure Tia Maria
1 measure full-fat milk or double cream

Serves 1
Prep time 2 minutes

1 Put half the cracked ice into a cocktail shaker and put the remaining cracked ice into a tall glass.

2 Add all the remaining ingredients to the shaker and shake until a frost forms on the outside of the shaker. Strain over the ice in the glass. Serve with a straw.

Cosmopolitan

MANY PEOPLE MAKE CLAIM ON BEING THE INVENTOR OF THE COSMOPOLITAN; HOWEVER, IT IS A RELATIVELY RECENT COCKTAIL THAT HAS BECOME SOMETHING OF A CLASSIC ALREADY.

1 Put the cracked ice into a cocktail shaker. Add all the remaining ingredients and shake until a frost forms on the outside of the shaker.

2 Strain into a chilled Martini (cocktail) glass. Decorate with an orange rind twist and serve.

6 ice cubes, cracked
1 measure vodka
½ measure Cointreau
1 measure cranberry juice
freshly squeezed juice of ½ lime
orange rind twist, to decorate

Serves 1
Prep time 2 minutes

TECHNIQUE: *Shaking*

Shaking is used to mix ingredients quickly and thoroughly and to chill the drink before serving.

Half-fill the cocktail shaker or the Boston glass (if using a Boston shaker) with ice cubes (or the amount specified in the recipe) or add cracked or crushed ice. If the recipe calls for a chilled glass, add a few ice cubes and some water to the glass and swirl them around before discarding. Add the remaining ingredients to the shaker. Put on the strainer and cap or, if using a Boston shaker, place the shaking tin over the glass. Shake until condensation forms on the outside of the shaker. Use both hands to hold either end of the shaker and to prevent it from slipping from your grip. The cocktail is then ready to be strained into the glass for serving by removing the cap but keeping the strainer in place.

TEQUILA SUNRISE LOLLIPOPS

V

125 ml (4 fl oz) lemon juice
125 g (4 oz) caster sugar
4 tablespoons tequila
125 ml (4 fl oz) soda water
1 tablespoon crème de cassis

WHEN YOU POUR THE CASSIS MIXTURE INTO THE MOULDS YOU WANT IT TO FLOAT ON TOP AND SLIGHTLY BLEND IN WITH THE TEQUILA BASE, SO THE TEQUILA NEEDS TO BE ALMOST FROZEN, BUT STILL A LITTLE SLUSHY.

Makes **4**
Prep time **10 minutes, plus freezing**
Cooking time **10 minutes**

1 Place the lemon juice and sugar in a saucepan with 125 ml (4 fl oz) water and slowly bring to the boil, allowing the sugar to dissolve. Leave to bubble for 5 minutes, then remove from the heat.

2 Pour in the tequila and soda water and mix well to combine. Measure out 6 tablespoons of the mixture and set aside. Divide the remaining mixture among four lollipop moulds. Place the moulds in the freezer for 4 hours.

3 Combine the reserved mixture with the cassis. After the 4 hours are up, remove the lollipops from the freezer and pour the cassis mixture into the moulds. Insert the lollipop sticks and freeze for another 4–6 hours until completely solid.

Avoiding A HANGOVER

You couldn't rightfully call yourself a student if you didn't overindulge on a regular basis. With student unions, local pubs and bars all keen to entice you inside to spend your overdrafts on cheap booze, the temptation is constant. So, there's little point preaching about the dangers of drink; instead, here's a few tried and tested ways to ease you into the morning after.

LINE YOUR STOMACH

The fact is that if you drink too much alcohol you'll pay for it the next day. But if you eat before you start knocking back the beers, you have a better chance of being able to remain standing by the end of the evening. Pasta is the obvious choice as it's full of slow-burning carbs that should help to soak up some of the alcohol. Other helpful hangover-busting ingredients include bread, eggs and milk.

DROWN YOUR SORROWS

If you alternate each alcoholic drink with a large glass of water, you'll not only keep your body hydrated (alcohol is dehydrating, which is partly to blame for the piercing headache the next morning) but you'll also slow down your alcohol consumption.

WALK IT OFF

If you spend your cab or bus money in the pub and end up having to walk home, you could actually be doing your hangover a favour. A brisk walk before you crash out in bed can help to start removing the alcohol from your system and you'll begin to sober up on the way home.

FORCE DOWN A FRY-UP

There's a good reason why people tuck into a full English breakfast when they're feeling the after-effects of a night on the tiles. Eggs contain an amino acid that can help to rid your body of toxins, while the fat and salt will replace vital minerals and should help to make you feel slightly more human.

BACK TO BED

Students are notoriously good at sleeping so take the opportunity to live up to your reputation and wipe out the day by staying in bed. Keep a bottle of water to hand so you can rehydrate between power naps and when the thought of food no longer makes you feel nauseous, try a plain piece of toast or a digestive biscuit to reacquaint your stomach with food.

CARROT, CHILLI & PINEAPPLE JUICE

250 g (8 oz) carrots
½ small chilli, deseeded
250 g (8 oz) pineapple, skinned and cored
ice cubes
juice of ½ lime
1 tablespoon chopped coriander leaves

Serves **1**
Prep time **10 minutes**

1 Juice the carrots with the chilli and pineapple. If you are using a blender, chop the vegetables and fruit into small pieces and pass through a sieve after blending.

2 Pour the juice into a glass over ice. Squeeze over the lime juice, stir in the chopped coriander and serve immediately.

MIXED BERRY SMOOTHIE

1 small ripe banana, roughly chopped
175 g (6 oz) fresh mixed berries, such as raspberries, blueberries and strawberries
250 ml (8 fl oz) vanilla bio yogurt
about 150 ml (¼ pint) milk

Serves **2**
Prep time **5 minutes**

1 Using a stick blender, or a food processor or blender if you have one, whizz the banana, berries, yogurt and milk and blend until thick and smooth, adding a little more milk if you prefer a thinner consistency.

2 Pour the smoothie into glasses and serve immediately.

CRANBERRY & APPLE SMOOTHIE

250 g (8 oz) apples
100 g ($3\frac{1}{2}$ oz) frozen cranberries
100 g ($3\frac{1}{2}$ oz) live natural yogurt
1 tablespoon clear honey
ice cubes (optional)

Serves 1
Prep time 5 minutes

1 Juice the apples. If you are using a blender, chop into small pieces and pass through a sieve after blending. Briefly blend the juice with the cranberries, yogurt and honey in a food processor or blender, or using a stick blender.

2 Pour the smoothie into a glass over ice, if using, and serve immediately.

Classic LEMONADE

125 ml (4 fl oz) sugar syrup (see below)
250 ml (8 fl oz) fresh lemon juice
lemon slices, to decorate

Serves 10
Prep time 10 minutes, plus chilling

1 Mix the ingredients with 1 litre ($1\frac{3}{4}$ pints) cold water in a bowl and stir very well. Transfer to an airtight container and chill thoroughly in the refrigerator. Stir regularly and drink within 3 days of preparing.

2 Serve in tall glasses, decorated with lemon slices.

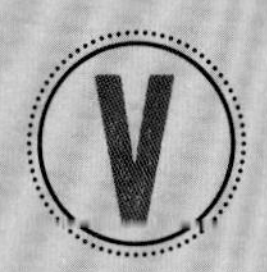

TECHNIQUE: *Sugar Syrup*

This is used as a sweetener in lots of cocktails and drinks. It blends into a cold drink more quickly than sugar and adds body. You can buy it in bottles, but it's very easy to make your own. Simply bring equal quantities of caster sugar and water to the boil in a small saucepan, stirring constantly, then boil for 1–2 minutes without stirring. Sugar syrup can be kept in a sterilized bottle in the fridge for up to 2 months.

ORANGE & RASPBERRY JUICE

1 Peel the oranges and divide the flesh into segments. Juice the orange segments with the raspberries. If you are using a blender, pass through a sieve after blending. Add the still water.

2 Pour the juice into tall glasses over ice, if using, and serve immediately.

2 large oranges
175 g (6 oz) raspberries
250 ml (8 fl oz) still water
ice cubes (optional)

Serves **2**
Prep time **5 minutes**

APPLE, APRICOT & PEACH JUICE

1 Juice the apples with the apricots and peach. If you are using a blender, chop the fruit into pieces and pass through a sieve after blending.

2 Blend the juice with a few ice cubes in a food processor or blender, or using a stick blender, for 10 seconds. Pour the juice into a glass, decorate with peach slices, if liked, and serve immediately.

2 apples
3 apricots, halved and stoned
1 peach, halved and stoned, plus extra to serve (optional)
ice cubes

Serves 1
Prep time **10 minutes**

FRUITY SUMMER *Milkshake*

1 ripe peach, halved, stoned and chopped
150 g (5 oz) strawberries, hulled
150 g (5 oz) raspberries
200 ml (7 fl oz) soya milk
ice cubes, to serve

Serves 2
Prep time 2 minutes

1 Using a stick blender, or a food processor or blender if you have one, blend the peach with the strawberries and raspberries to a smooth purée, scraping the mixture down from the sides of the bowl if necessary.

2 Add the soya milk and blend the ingredients again until the mixture is smooth and frothy. Pour the milkshake over the ice cubes in tall glasses.

V

BANANA LASSI

3 ripe bananas, roughly chopped
500 g (17 oz) natural yogurt
1–2 tablespoons caster sugar
¼ teaspoon ground cardamom seeds, plus extra for decorating (optional)

Serves 4
Preparation time 10 minutes

1 Put all the ingredients in a food processor or blender and blend until smooth.

2 Pour into tall glasses and serve chilled, decorated with extra cardamom seeds if liked. This makes an ideal breakfast drink.

VEGETABLE STOCK

YOU CAN USE ALMOST ANY MIXTURE OF VEGETABLES, BUT THEY MUST BE REALLY FRESH. MAKE SURE YOU INCLUDE SOME ONION, BUT OMIT VEGETABLES WITH STRONG FLAVOURS SUCH AS CABBAGE AND STARCHY ONES LIKE POTATOES WHICH WILL MAKE THE STOCK CLOUDY. FOR A DARK STOCK, LEAVE THE SKINS ON THE ONIONS AND USE PLENTY OF MUSHROOMS.

1 tablespoon vegetable oil
2 onions, roughly chopped
2 carrots, roughly chopped
2 celery sticks, roughly chopped
500 g (1 lb) mixture other vegetables, such as parsnips, fennel, leeks, courgettes, mushrooms and tomatoes
1 bouquet garni
1 teaspoon black peppercorns

Makes **about 1 litre (1¾ pints)**
Prep time **10 minutes**
Cooking time **50 minutes**

1 Heat the oil in a large heavy-based saucepan and gently fry all the vegetables for 5 minutes. Add 1.5 litres (2½ pints) cold water, the bouquet garni and peppercorns and bring slowly to the boil.

2 Reduce the heat and simmer the stock very gently for 40 minutes, skimming the surface from time to time if necessary.

3 Strain the stock through a large sieve, preferably a conical one, and leave to cool. Don't squeeze the juice out of the vegetables or the stock will be cloudy.

4 Leave the stock to cool completely, then chill.

Veggie Gravy

1 tablespoon vegetable oil
2 onions, sliced
2 teaspoons caster sugar
250 ml (8 fl oz) stout
150 ml (¼ pint) Vegetable Stock (see above)
salt and pepper

Serves **4**
Prep time **5 minutes**
Cooking time **10 minutes**

1 Heat the oil in a frying pan, add the onions and sugar and fry for about 5 minutes until deep golden.

2 Add the beer and stock, then season to taste with salt and pepper. Cook for 5 minutes, stirring frequently.

TOMATO SAUCE

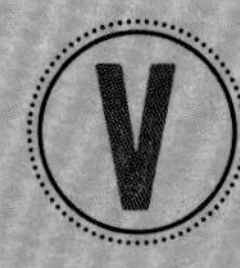

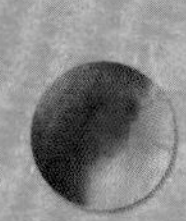

3 tablespoons vegetable oil
2 red onions, finely sliced
2 garlic cloves, crushed and chopped
2 x 400 g (13 oz) cans chopped tomatoes
1 teaspoon red wine vinegar
pinch of sugar
salt and pepper

Serves **4**
Prep time **5 minutes**
Cooking time **15 minutes**

1 Heat the oil in a large saucepan, add the onions and garlic and fry for 3 minutes.

2 Add the tomatoes, vinegar, sugar and a dash of salt and pepper and simmer until reduced to a rich tomato sauce.

Béchamel Sauce

300 ml (½ pint) full-fat milk
½ small onion
1 bay leaf
½ teaspoon peppercorns
3–4 parsley stalks
15 g (½ oz) butter
15 g (½ oz) plain flour
pinch of grated nutmeg
salt and pepper

Serves 4
Prep time 10 minutes, plus infusing
Cooking time 10 minutes

1 Put the milk in a saucepan with the onion, bay leaf, peppercorns and parsley stalks and bring almost to the boil. Remove the pan from the heat and leave to infuse for 20 minutes. Strain the milk through a sieve into a jug.

2 Melt the butter in a heavy-based saucepan until bubbling. Tip in the flour and stir quickly to combine. Cook the mixture gently, stirring constantly with a wooden spoon, for 1–2 minutes to make a smooth, pale roux.

3 Remove the pan from the heat and gradually whisk in the warm milk, stirring constantly until the sauce is completely smooth. Return the pan to a medium heat and cook, stirring, until the sauce comes to the boil.

4 Reduce the heat to low and continue to cook the sauce for about 5 minutes, stirring frequently until it is smooth and glossy and thinly coats the back of the spoon. Season to taste with salt, pepper and plenty of grated nutmeg.

RICH CHEESE SAUCE

THIS SMOOTH AND CREAMY CHEESE SAUCE IS BOTH SIMPLE AND DELICIOUS, AND IDEAL FOR USING UP LEFTOVER CHEESE. YOU CAN VARY THE RECIPE WITH PIECES OF GRUYÈRE OR STILTON, OR COMBINE SEVERAL DIFFERENT CHEESES.

300 ml (½ pint) full-fat milk
½ small onion
1 bay leaf
15 g (½ oz) butter
15 g (½ oz) plain flour
1 teaspoon green peppercorns in brine, rinsed and drained
75 g (3 oz) mature Cheddar cheese, grated
15 g (½ oz) Parmesan-style cheese, grated
pinch of grated nutmeg
salt

Serves 4
Prep time **10 minutes, plus infusing**
Cooking time **10 minutes**

1 Follow steps 1, 2 and 3 of Béchamel Sauce (see page 247), omitting the black peppercorns and parsley.

2 Using a pestle and mortar, lightly crush the green peppercorns until they are broken into small pieces. Alternatively, put them in a plastic food bag and crush with the back of a spoon. Add them to the sauce with the cheeses and a little nutmeg. Cook over a gentle heat, stirring frequently, for about 5 minutes until smooth and glossy. Adjust the seasoning and serve hot.

PARSLEY SAUCE

15 g (½ oz) curly parsley
250 ml (8 fl oz) Vegetable Stock (see page 246)
25 g (1 oz) butter
25 g (1 oz) plain flour
250 ml (8 fl oz) full-fat milk
3 tablespoons single cream
salt and pepper

Serves 4
Prep time **10 minutes**
Cooking time **10 minutes**

1 Discard any tough stalks from the parsley and blend with half the stock in a food processor or blender, or using a stick blender. Blend until the parsley is very finely chopped.

2 Melt the butter in a heavy-based saucepan until bubbling. Tip in the flour and stir quickly to combine. Cook the mixture gently, stirring constantly with a wooden spoon, for 2 minutes.

3 Remove the pan from the heat and gradually whisk in the parsley-flavoured stock, then the remaining stock, until smooth. Whisk in the milk. Return to the heat and bring to the boil, stirring. Reduce the heat and continue to cook the sauce for about 5 minutes, stirring frequently, until it is smooth and glossy. The sauce should thinly coat the back of the spoon.

4 Stir in the cream and a little salt and pepper and heat gently to warm through.

PESTO

PESTO IS QUICK AND EASY TO MAKE IN A FOOD PROCESSOR, BUT IF YOU DON'T HAVE ONE, TRYING BLENDING THE INGREDIENTS IN SMALL BATCHES USING A STICK BLENDER. FRESHLY MADE PESTO HAS NUMEROUS USES, MOST COMMONLY AS A PASTA SAUCE BUT ALSO TO FLAVOUR SOUPS, STEWS AND RISOTTOS.

50 g (2 oz) basil, including stalks
50 g (2 oz) pine nuts
65 g (2½ oz) Parmesan-style cheese, grated
2 garlic cloves, chopped
125 ml (4 fl oz) olive oil
salt

1 Tear the basil into pieces and put it into a food processor with the pine nuts, Parmesan and garlic.

2 Blend lightly until the nuts and cheese are broken into small pieces, scraping the mixture down from the sides of the bowl if necessary.

3 Add the olive oil and a little salt and blend to a thick paste. Stir into freshly cooked pasta or turn into a bowl and refrigerate. It can be kept, covered, for up to 5 days.

Serves **4**
Prep time **5 minutes**

To make Red Pesto, drain 125g (4 oz) sun-dried tomatoes in oil, chop them into small pieces and add to the food processor instead of the basil.

APPLE SAUCE

THE SECRET OF A GOOD APPLE SAUCE IS TO USE PLENTY OF BUTTER AND LET THE APPLES AND FLAVOURINGS COOK VERY SLOWLY.

50 g (2 oz) unsalted butter
3 large cooking apples, peeled, cored and chopped
50 g (2 oz) caster sugar
6 whole cloves
finely grated rind and juice of 1 lemon
salt

Serves 6
Prep time 10 minutes
Cooking time 20 minutes

1 Melt the butter in a heavy-based saucepan. Add the apples, sugar, cloves, lemon rind and juice and a little salt.

2 Cover the pan with a lid and leave to cook gently over the lowest heat for about 20 minutes, stirring the mixture occasionally, until the apples are very soft and mushy. Adjust the seasoning, adding a little more lemon juice for a tangier flavour, if liked. Transfer to a jug and serve warm or cold.

GLOSSY CHOCOLATE SAUCE

USE A GOOD-QUALITY DARK CHOCOLATE WITH ABOUT 70 PER CENT COCOA SOLIDS TO GIVE THIS SAUCE A RICH FLAVOUR AND PLENTY OF SHEEN. TAKE CARE NOT TO OVERHEAT THE CHOCOLATE OR THE SAUCE WILL DEVELOP A GRAINY TEXTURE.

125 g (4 oz) caster sugar
200 g (7 oz) plain dark chocolate, chopped
25 g (1 oz) unsalted butter

Serves 5–6
Prep time 5 minutes
Cooking time 2–3 minutes

1 Put the sugar in a small heavy-based saucepan and add 125 ml (4 fl oz) water. Cook over a low heat, stirring constantly with a wooden spoon, until the sugar has dissolved.

2 Bring the syrup to the boil and boil for 1 minute, then remove the pan from the heat and leave to cool for 1 minute. Tip the chocolate into the pan.

3 Add the butter and leave until the chocolate and butter have melted, stirring frequently, until the sauce is smooth and glossy. If the last of the chocolate doesn't melt completely or you want to serve the sauce warm, return the pan briefly to the lowest heat setting.

Buttercream

100 g (3½ oz) unsalted butter, softened
150 g (5 oz) icing sugar

Makes **enough for an 18–20 cm (7–8 inch) cake**
Prep time **3 minutes**

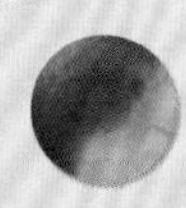

For a coffee-flavoured alternative, dissolve 1 tablespoon instant espresso powder in 2 teaspoons boiling water and beat into the buttercream.

THE BEST BUTTERCREAM IS VERY SOFT AND FLUFFY WITH A FLAVOUR THAT'S NOT TOO OVERPOWERINGLY SWEET.

1 Beat the butter in a bowl with a little of the sugar until smooth.

2 Add the remaining sugar and beat until pale and fluffy. Add a few drops of boiling water and beat for a few moments more.

Cream Cheese FROSTING

THIS IS A LOVELY TANGY FROSTING WITH PLENTY OF FLAVOUR, AND IT'S GREAT FOR ANYONE WHO DOESN'T LIKE INTENSELY SUGARY SPREADS. TASTE FOR SWEETNESS ONCE IT'S WHISKED – YOU CAN EASILY BEAT IN ANOTHER 25 G (1 OZ) SUGAR IF IT'S NOT SWEET ENOUGH.

200 g (7 oz) full-fat cream cheese
1–2 teaspoons lime or lemon juice
75 g (3 oz) icing sugar

Makes **enough for an 18–20 cm (7–8 inch) cake**
Prep time **3 minutes**

1 Beat the cream cheese in a bowl until it is softened and smooth. Beat in 1 teaspoon of the juice.

2 Add the icing sugar and beat until smooth, adding a little more juice if the mixture is very firm.

INDEX

apples
apple, apricot & peach juice 244
apple sauce 250
cranberry & apple smoothie 243
fruity baked apples 229
toffee apple bake 226
apricots
apple, apricot & peach juice 244
pumpkin seed & apricot muesli 12
summer fruits with honeyed oat topping 212
aubergines
aubergine cannelloni 149
aubergine pâté 141
butternut & aubergine tikka 65
chickpea & aubergine tagine 42
flash-in-the-pan ratatouille 138
melanzane parmagiana 68
ribbon pasta with aubergines & pine nuts 155
tortillas with minted chilli & aubergine yoghurt 163
warm aubergine salad 192
avocados
sweetcorn cakes with avocado salsa 108
tricolore avocado & couscous salad 110

bananas
banana lassi 245
banoffee layers 215
mixed berry smoothie 242
vegan banana pecan cake with caramel topping 96
beans
bean & potato moussaka 66
black bean soup with soba noodles 181
butter bean & vegetable nut crumble 73
butter bean & vegetable soup 28
Cheddar burgers with cucumber salsa 121
cheesy lentil & vegetable pie 77
chimichurri chips & beans 175
corn & bean tortilla stack 112
gardener's pie 54
garlic & bean pâté 204
baked peppers with goats' cheese 62
healthy green bean & broccoli salad 188
hearty minestrone 26
Massaman vegetable curry 36
mixed bean kedgeree 139
nut koftas with minted yoghurt 115
red beans with coconut & cashews 40
ricotta & broad bean fritters 116
root vegetable & bean crumble 76
smokey bean & cheese burgers 120
spicy Mexican wraps 162
vegetable noodles in spiced coconut milk 177
warm pasta salad with lemon & broccoli 193
béchamel sauce 247
beer & barley stew with dumplings 45
beetroot
beetroot risotto with horseradish & mixed leaves 169
couscous fritters with beetroot 117
red cabbage & beetroot lentils 205
red cabbage coleslaw 206
berries
berry, honey & yoghurt pots 10
blackberry muffin slice 92
freezing 92
instant summer berry sorbet 210
mixed berry smoothie 242
blueberry & lemon pancakes 16
bread 51, 114
cheat's Mediterranean focaccia 88
choc cinnamon eggy bread 233
Middle Eastern bread salad 189
mixed seed soda bread 91
mustard rarebit 202
panzanella 191
spiced flatbreads 90
Swiss cheese melts 161
broccoli
broccoli & blue cheese souffles 64
broccoli & spinach eggahs 63
healthy green bean & broccoli salad 188
tagliatelle with blue cheese
butter 153
warm pasta salad with lemon & broccoli 193
budgeting 4-5
bulgar wheat
bulgar wheat with goats' cheese & red onion 111
feta-stuffed peppers 61
stuffed red onions 60
tabbouleh with fruit & nuts 196
buttercream 95, 251
butternut squash
butternut & aubergine tikka 65
Thai green vegetable curry 130

cabbage
cheesy lentil & vegetable pie 77
chunky peanut roast with homemade coleslaw 69
red cabbage & beetroot lentils 205
red cabbage coleslaw 206
cakes
blackberry muffin slice 92
chocolate fridge cake 222
chocolate fudge cake 97
lemon drizzle cake 94
lemon popping candy cakes 98
vegan banana pecan cake with caramel topping 96
Victoria sandwich cake 95
Camembert wraps with hot pepper salsa 164
carbohydrates 179
carrots
carrot & feta potato cakes 172
carrot, chilli & pineapple juice 242
cheesy lentil & vegetable pie 77
root vegetable & bean crumble 76
Thai green vegetable curry 130
cauliflower
buttered cauliflower crumble 52
potato, cauliflower & spinach curry 37
romesco cauliflower cheese 53
tricolore cauliflower gratin 71
cheese
aubergine cannelloni 149
bean & potato moussaka 66
broccoli & blue cheese souffles 64
bulgar wheat with goats' cheese & red onion 111
butter bean & vegetable nut crumble 73

buttered cauliflower crumble 52
Camembert wraps with hot pepper salsa 164
carrot & feta potato cakes 172
chargrilled polenta triangles 201
Cheddar burgers with cucumber salsa 121
cheese & herb scones 87
cheese, tomato & basil muffins 86
cheesy lentil & vegetable pie 77
creamy courgette orzo pasta 132
creamy mushroom & tarragon rigatoni 154
feta-stuffed peppers 61
filo, pesto & mozzarella parcels 79
gardener's pie 54
gnocchi with sage butter 56
goats' cheese & pepper lasagne 144
goats' cheese linguine 156
griddled Greek-style sandwiches 118
baked peppers with goats' cheese 62
haloumi & rocket carbonara 148
haloumi with pomegranate salsa 124
kale & pesto linguine 134
leek & mushroom pasties 81
lentil & parsnip cottage pie 47
macaroni cheese with spinach 159
Margherita tart 84
melanzane parmagiana 68
mushroom, courgette & mascarpone lasagne 146
mustard rarebit 202
red onion & goats' cheese tart 82
red onion, rosemary & gruyère toad 70
rich cheese sauce 248
ricotta & broad bean fritters 116
romesco cauliflower cheese 53
root vegetable & bean crumble 76
smokey bean & cheese burgers 120
spicy Mexican wraps 162
spinach & potato gratin 72
spinach & potato tortilla 123
spring onion, dill & chive pancakes 122
strawberry cheesecake mug cake 224
stuffed red onions 60
sweet potato, rocket & haloumi salad 190
Swiss cheese melts 161
tagliatelle with blue cheese butter 153
tricolore avocado & couscous salad 110
tricolore cauliflower gratin 71
veggie carbonara 147
chickpeas
chickpea & aubergine tagine 42
chickpea purée with eggs & spiced oil 38
falafel cakes 114
tomato & chickpea stew 44
choc cinnamon eggy bread 233
chocolate
chocolate chip cookies 102
chocolate fridge cake 222
chocolate fromage frais 219
chocolate fudge cake 97
chocolate mocha brownies 100
glossy chocolate sauce 250
quick tiramisu 220
rich chocolate mousse 223
syrupy pears with chocolate crumble 227
cocktails 236-9
coffee
buttercream 251
chocolate mocha brownies 100
quick tiramisu 220
coleslaw, red cabbage 206
Cosmopolitan 238
courgettes
corn & courgette cakes 200
courgette & creamy tomato penne 152
creamy courgette orzo pasta 132
flash-in-the-pan ratatouille 138
hot and spicy vegetable noodles 180
mushroom, courgette & mascarpone lasagne 146
veggie carbonara 147
couscous
couscous fritters with beetroot 117
couscous salad 137
tricolore avocado & couscous salad 110
cranberries
cranberry & apple smoothie 243
cranberry, oatmeal & cinnamon scones 105
cream cheese frosting 251
cucumber
Cheddar burgers with cucumber salsa 121
Middle Eastern bread salad 189

dinners with mates 74-5

eggs
broccoli & blue cheese souffles 64
broccoli & spinach eggahs 63
carrot & feta potato cakes 172
chickpea purée with eggs & spiced oil 38
choc cinnamon eggy bread 233
gado gado salad 187
garlic & paprika soup with a floating egg 140
mixed bean kedgeree 139
mushroom & egg fried rice 194
mushroom, egg & cress all-day pizza 160
oven-baked sausage brunch 23
pesto scrambled eggs 19
potato rösti with frazzled eggs 22
potato tortilla 207
spinach & potato tortilla 123
tomato, pepper & egg tortillas 18

falafel cakes 114
fennel
pasta with fennel & rocket 158
feta-stuffed peppers 61
frozen food 7, 42, 92, 114
stickers on 212

gado gado salad 187
gardener's pie 54
gingery grilled tofu with noodles 127
gnocchi with sage butter 56

hangovers 240-1
health and food safety 5-6
healthy eating 178-9
horseradish
beetroot risotto with horseradish & mixed leaves 169

Jamaican coconut curry 176

kale
kale & pesto linguine 134
rice pilaf with kale crisps 165

leeks
leek & mushroom pasties 81
new potato, coriander & leek soup 31
leftovers 50-1, 137
lemons
blueberry & lemon pancakes 16
classic lemonade 243
lemon & herb risotto 170
lemon & spinach soup 32
lemon drizzle cake 94
lemon popping candy cakes 98
warm pasta salad with lemon & broccoli 193
lentils
cheesy lentil & vegetable pie 77
green lentil soup with spiced butter 30
lentil & parsnip cottage pie 47
lentil bolognese 48
lentil dhal with potato chapatis 34
red cabbage & beetroot lentils 205
spicy lentil & tomato soup 29
limes
pineapple with lime & chilli syrup 218
vegan chilli & lime chocolate muffins 99
lunches 136-7

mangoes
mango & mint carpaccio 216
mango curry 131
Margherita tart 84
markets 21, 179, 206
Massaman vegetable curry 36
menu planning 21
Middle Eastern bread salad 189
minestrone, hearty 26
mojito 237
muddling 237
mushrooms
aubergine pâté 141
creamy mushroom & chive risotto 166
creamy mushroom & tarragon rigatoni 154
leek & mushroom pasties 81
lentil & parsnip cottage pie 47
mushroom & egg fried rice 194
mushroom, courgette & mascarpone lasagne 146
mushroom, egg & cress all-day pizza 160
mushroom tagliatelle with gremolata 150
oven-baked sausage brunch 23
spinach & mushroom ramen 129
stuffed red onions 60
vegetable noodles in spiced coconut milk 177
warm mushrooms with potato rosti 174

noodles
black bean soup with soba noodles 181
five-minute pad thai 126
gingery grilled tofu with noodles 127
hot and spicy vegetable noodles 180
rice noodle pancakes with stir-fried vegetables 182
spinach & mushroom ramen 129
vegetable noodles in spiced coconut milk 177

oats
chewy oat & raisin bars 103
cranberry, oatmeal & cinnamon scones 105
crumbly raspberry & oat slices 104
summer fruits with honeyed oat topping 212
okra & coconut stew 41
onions 7
bulgar wheat with goats' cheese & red onion 111
potato & onion pizza 57
red onion & goats' cheese tart 82
red onion, rosemary & gruyère toad 70
stuffed red onions 60
veggie gravy 246
orange & raspberry juice 244

pancakes
blueberry & lemon pancakes 16
buckwheat pancakes 17
spring onion, dill & chive pancakes 122
panzanella 191
parsley sauce 248
parsnips
crisp parsnip cakes 199
curried parsnip soup 27
lentil & parsnip cottage pie 47
root vegetable & bean crumble 76
passionfruit
nutty passionfruit yoghurts 214
pasta 7, 192
aubergine cannelloni 149
courgette & creamy tomato penne 152
creamy courgette orzo pasta 132
creamy mushroom & tarragon rigatoni 154
garlic & paprika soup with a floating egg 140
goats' cheese & pepper lasagne 144
goats' cheese linguine 156
haloumi & rocket carbonara 148
hearty minestrone 26
kale & pesto linguine 134
leftover 51
macaroni cheese with spinach 159
mushroom, courgette & mascarpone lasagne 146
mushroom tagliatelle with gremolata 150
pasta with fennel & rocket 158
ribbon pasta with aubergines & pine nuts 155
spaghetti with garlic & black pepper 135
tagliatelle with blue cheese butter 153
veggie carbonara 147
warm pasta salad with lemon & broccoli 193
peaches
almost instant peach trifle 221
apple, apricot & peach juice 244
fruity summer milkshake 245
peanuts
chunky peanut roast with homemade coleslaw 69
pearl barley
beer & barley stew with dumplings 45
pears
syrupy pears with chocolate crumble 227
peas
easy pea risotto 168
peppers
Camembert wraps with hot pepper salsa 164
feta stuffed peppers 61
goats' cheese & pepper lasagne 144
baked peppers with goats' cheese 62
okra & coconut stew 41
panzanella 191
tomato, pepper & egg tortillas 18
pesto 249
Pimm's cocktail 236
pineapple
carrot, chilli & pineapple juice 242
pineapple with lime & chilli syrup 218
plums
warm spiced plums 228
polenta
chargrilled polenta triangles 201

pomegranates
haloumi with pomegranate salsa 124
potatoes
bean & potato moussaka 66
carrot & feta potato cakes 172
chunky potato chips 207
gnocchi with sage butter 56
leftover 51
lentil dhal with potato chapatis 34
new potato, coriander & leek soup 31
potato & onion pizza 57
potato, cauliflower & spinach curry 37
potato rösti with frazzled eggs 22
spinach & potato gratin 72
spinach & potato tortilla 123
tempeh balti 35
warm mushrooms with potato rosti 174
pumpkin seed & apricot muesli 12

quinoa porridge with raspberries 14

raspberries
crumbly raspberry & oat slices 104
fruity summer milkshake 245
orange & raspberry juice 244
quinoa porridge with raspberries 14
rhubarb & raspberry crumble 230
ratatouille, flash-in-the-pan 138
rhubarb & raspberry crumble 230
rice 7, 51
beetroot risotto with horseradish & mixed leaves 169
creamy mushroom & chive risotto 166
easy pea risotto 168
lemon & herb risotto 170
mixed bean kedgeree 139
mushroom & egg fried rice 194
rice pilaf with kale crisps 165
sage & tomato pilaf 171

sandwiches 136, 137
sangria 236
sauces 247-50
shopping 20-1, 21, 73, 126, 168, 180, 194
online 20, 73
shopping lists 75
snacks 137
spices 7
spinach
broccoli & spinach eggahs 63
goats' cheese & pepper lasagne 144
hot and spicy vegetable noodles 180
lemon & spinach soup 32
macaroni cheese with spinach 159
potato, cauliflower & spinach curry 37
spinach & mushroom ramen 129
spinach & potato gratin 72
spinach & potato tortilla 123
tempeh balti 35
tricolore cauliflower gratin 71
strawberries
fruity summer milkshake 245
strawberry cheesecake mug cake 224
strawberry crush 213
summer fruits with honeyed oat topping 212
sugar syrup 243
sweet potatoes
baked sweet potatoes 198
chimichurri chips & beans 175
Moroccan-style sweet potato pie 78
sweet potato & garlic mash 197
sweet potato, rocket & haloumi salad 190
sweetcorn
corn & bean tortilla stack 112
corn & courgette cakes 200
okra & coconut stew 41
sweetcorn cakes with avocado salsa 108

tabbouleh with fruit & nuts 196
tempeh balti 35
tequila sunrise lollipops 239
tofu
gingery grilled tofu with noodles 127
stir-fried tofu with basil & chilli 128
tofu, cinnamon & honey parcels 80
tomatoes
cheat's Mediterranean focaccia 88
cheese, tomato & basil muffins 86
cherry tomato tarts with pesto crème fraîche 85
courgette & creamy tomato penne 152
feta-stuffed peppers 61
Margherita tart 84
melanzane parmagiana 68
Middle Eastern bread salad 189
oven-baked sausage brunch 23
panzanella 191
sage & tomato pilaf 171
spicy lentil & tomato soup 29
spinach & potato gratin 72
tomato & chickpea stew 44
tomato, pepper & egg tortillas 18
tomato sauce 247
tortillas
Camembert wraps with hot pepper salsa 164
corn & bean tortilla stack 112
potato tortilla 207
spicy Mexican wraps 162
tomato, pepper & egg tortillas 18
tortillas with minted chilli & aubergine yoghurt 163
treacle sponge microwave puddings 225

vegetable stock 246
vegetables
five-minute pad thai 126
leftover 51
noodle pancakes with stir-fried vegetables 182
shopping for 28, 206
vegetable noodles in spiced coconut milk 177
Victoria sandwich cake 95

White Russian 238-9

yoghurt
banana lassi 245
berry, honey & yoghurt pots 10
butternut & aubergine tikka 65
instant summer berry sorbet 210
nut koftas with minted yoghurt 115
nutty passionfruit yoghurts 214
ricotta & broad bean fritters 116
tortillas with minted chilli & aubergine yoghurt 163

ACKNOWLEDGEMENTS

Picture Credits
Octopus Publishing Group Stephen Conroy 72, 93, 95, 97, 101, 102, 104, 131, 145, 149, 151, 187, 203, 204, 215, 218, 222, 225, 228, 231, 236, 238, 245, 249; Will Heap 11, 26, 53, 64, 109, 110, 113, 122, 123, 130, 133, 134, 138, 139, 193, 200, 210, 217; William Lingwood 213; David Munns 219, 233; Lis Parsons 68, 147, 239, 242 above; William Reavell 17, 29, 33, 39, 40, 44, 49, 55, 57, 85, 105, 111, 115, 140, 154, 155, 157, 161, 163, 169, 174, 177, 181, 183, 191, 196, 221, 227; Gareth Sambidge 16, 62, 63, 87, 229; William Shaw 13, 15, 23, 27, 28, 37, 41, 43, 47, 61, 67, 71, 75, 81, 83, 84, 89, 90, 98, 103, 119, 125, 127, 135, 152, 158, 159, 167, 171, 173, 188, 195, 205, 211, 242 below; Ian Wallace 19, 22, 46, 56, 86, 91, 128, 189, 198, 201, 223; **Shutterstock** Anneka 136; Beauty photographer 74; BlueOrange Studio 21 above; cluckva 14 background; designelements 87 background; Gencho Petkov 47 background; Goran Bogicevic 5 above; HLPhoto 51 below; Martin Parratt 179 below; MShev 137; Nejron Photo 4 below, 20, 240; pcruciatti 179 above; pepmibastock 3 background; photastic 12 background, 81 background; primopiano 65 background; Quanthem 21 below; taviphoto 79 background; The_Pixel 10 background; vetkit 2 background; worker 16 background; YanLev 3 below; Yulia Davidovich 51 above, 178; Zeljko Bozic 180 background. **Thinkstock** Hemera Technologies 31 background; kyoshino 4 background; Milos Luzanin 18 background; Nastco 32 background.

Publisher Sarah Ford
Editor Pauline Bache
Features Writer Cara Frost-Sharratt
Designers Eoghan O'Brien and Jaz Bahra
Picture Library Manager Jennifer Veall
Assistant Production Controller
Meskerem Berhane